"*Holding On Loosely* grips you tightly. You can't help but catch the scent of personal familiarity in this deeply honest and intimately revealing story of Pablo's pursuit of acceptance and ultimate freedom to be who he was created to be—truly beloved."

Michael L. Simpson

Executive Coach with Trove, Inc., and Best-Selling Author of

Permission Evangelism and *I Believe, Now What?*

"Truth at its best is profoundly simple and often an invitation to live courageously, powerfully, humbly. *Holding On Loosely* is such an invitation. Exuding truth gained from the remarkable life of the author, this book creatively portrays what we all need the courage to do daily: hold on loosely. Pablo's story is not a quick-fix or easy-answer book. It will challenge you to examine where you are in over control in your own life—even where you think you are not in that mode. Pablo's book came to me at a time when I needed its truth to help me refocus and renew my commitment to living life as God intends me to live it. Now this book is in your own hands right on time, no matter your circumstances."

Wes Roberts

Author, Founder of Leadership Design Group

"Our desire to control the world around us often drives our behaviors; yet our inability to achieve that control brings about a fear-based mindset which actually controls us. *Holding On Loosely* is more than just a concept. It is a glimpse of one man's journey from perceived control to real release. We are invited to walk alongside Pablo as God reveals the deep truths that changed his life and can change yours as well. Pablo dispenses of the religious rhetoric that often dominates the typical Christian self-help books, and he promotes the truth about our invitation to intimate relationship with God. What He has given freely we need only receive. Don't be surprised if you open the front cover with one perspective and close the back cover with a whole new revelation. This is a must-read!"

Mitch Salmon
Founder, Behind the Curtain Ministries and Fisher of Men Productions

"*Holding On Loosely* will change you. It will leave you wanting to experience the God who never lets go and who made you to enjoy His love in the moment and for all of eternity."

Krista White
Professional Sports Mentor on the WTA Tour

"There are stories that entertain and stories that inspire...but then there are a few stories that awaken something deep inside our heart that is good and noble. This is one of those stories. A true story about a man who is not unlike you and me. You won't have to commit to finishing *Holding On Loosely*—it will engage you till the end."

Gary Barkalow
Founder, The Noble Heart, Colorado Springs, CO
Author, *It's Your Call: What Are You Doing Here?*

"This drama is played out on center court, where an enlightened tennis coach sees the real battle his player is struggling against: the weight of performance she carries from her father. The only way the coach can help her is to shake his own opponent that he has lost to year after year, *religious oppression*. This story gives you a front-row seat to the final match between freedom and bondage."

Jeff Andrechyn
Captain, US Airways
Founder, Expeditions of the Heart

"Swinging wide the door of his life, Pablo courageously exposes us to his very personal and powerful journey. He leads us through the corridors of both triumph and pain, but one always emerges with a sense of possibility and hope. Pablo's honesty, tempered with humor, gives us permission to expose our pain to the healing hand of the Father with a smile on our face! A compelling read that just might change your life!"

Malcolm Baxter
Pastor, Cape Town, South Africa

"*Holding On Loosely* is a journey of gripping onto God in everything, relinquishing control of your life through His loving embrace, and peacefully living in the 'Zone' of His presence. This book will inspire you as Pablo authentically reveals the mystery and majesty of God through a surrendered life. I heartily recommend this book. It will plant a desire in every reader to hold on loosely and live presently in the zone for which they have been born."

Robert Ricciardelli
Founder, Converging Zone Network

HOLDING ON LOOSELY

Finding Life in the Beautiful Tension

HOLDING ON LOOSELY

Finding Life in the Beautiful Tension

PABLO GIACOPELLI

HEART & LIFE
PUBLISHERS

Holding On Loosely: Finding Life in the Beautiful Tension

Published by Heart & Life Publishers, Grand Rapids, Michigan.
www.heartandlife.com.

ISBN-10: 0-9839924-0-0
ISBN-13: 978-0-9839924-0-0

Unless otherwise noted, Scripture taken from *THE MESSAGE*, Copyright © 1993, 1994, 1995, 1996, 2000, 2001, 2002. Used by permission of NavPress Publishing Group.

Cover design: Nole Design
Cover photo: Urmas Liiv
Interior design: Frank Gutbrod

Printed in the United States of America

I dedicate this book to my precious wife, Madeleine,

and my wonderful children, Vanessa, Jake, Mia and Gisella.

May you always hold on loosely to life

and tightly to the One who gave it to you.

CONTENTS

To all those I have worked with, coached and competed against; to all my colleagues, the night staff at hotels where I stayed, the housekeeping staff of the rooms I occupied, the chair and line umpires, tournament staff, and airline personnel I encountered; and to my family and God.

A part of me hesitates to publish this book. I fear that how I have acted and treated people on occasion should be counted against me and my intended message. Admittedly, there is a gap between how I would like to respond to the world and treat others and the personal reality I wake up to on any given morning.

The opposite of grace is not *un-grace.* The opposite of grace is *karma*; the world lives by the wisdom of karma, or, *what comes around, goes around.* While I believe it is true that our actions and reactions influence our world for bad or for good (a form of karma), I owe my life to the generosity of grace. My failings are not the end of the story; in the truest sense of grace, I live in the unmerited favor of a God who returns good for evil, kindness for unkindness and salvation for crucifixion. I have moved past karma into grace. I choose to live my life as a conduit of that grace from Christ to the world and to you.

You and I are beloved children of God. In light of that true identity, I pray that all of us will claim our heritage and spend our Father's riches on a world thirsty for grace.

Today I am living a new way, and this path is leading me through forgiveness, reconciliation and grace. To those I have failed to love well on my journey: May we find time very soon to mend the broken places by the love and grace of God.

—Pablo

FOREWORD

In life we are all on a journey. This journey can sometimes be very satisfying and an adventure full of wonderful surprises. Most of us would love to live a life like this, which goes from peak to peak avoiding all the valleys in between.

Though we are promised from public platforms, many books, and a multitude of movies, that such a plain-sailing life is possible (though I have yet to meet someone who has actually experienced it), we all know that our best-dream life devoid of any dark days simply does not exist. Jesus himself never promised such a thing when He reminded us that there would be trouble in this life.

Holding On Loosely is more than just a book about a tennis coach finding a way to walk with God without feeling guilty all of the time. It is a tool, a way to approach this walk called life. It is a philosophy closely knitted to the way I believe Jesus chose to live His life both internally and externally while He was here on earth with us.

Let's face it, we will all go through and experience suffering and difficult times along the way. This is part of life and part of what we are all exposed to while living under the sun. Trying to avoid this darker side of reality, pretending that we can go through life without its ever casting a shadow on us, is the same as a tennis player thinking he can win a Grand Slam without having to win seven matches and face feelings of fear, insecurity, worry, anxiety and failure each time he steps onto a court.

The fact is that all who win Grand Slams face these invisible adversaries and overcome them if they want to succeed. Most don't face them, and even fewer overcome them. The few who do are somehow able to play the game without appearing affected at all from the foes that kill the rest of the field. Yet though they seem unaffected, they are challenged; they just have found a way to keep walking one step at a time and still win.

Holding On Loosely will help you adopt such a mindset. It is not a tips-and-tricks manual that will absolve you from reality or the pain and suffering we all have to undergo. It will, however, help you to walk through the valleys and experience, not merely remember, that the promise of God "to never leave us nor forsake us" is indeed really, really true. *Holding On Loosely* will help you stay present to where God is instead of living constantly in the future or the past.

You will learn to focus on the process—or as Jesus said, to live one day at a time instead of driving yourself crazy trying to control, manipulate and fix your life and the lives of others. You will find freedom from the constant pressure to succeed in order to prove to God and the world that you are worthy to be loved.

Imagine closing your eyes at any given moment, asking, "God who are you," and feeling His overwhelming presence. Wouldn't it be great to know this presence while you were at work or at the bus station, or maybe while you faced the possibility of bankruptcy or the loss of a loved one? This is what *Holding On Loosely* is about: becoming aware that we are in His presence, where both our lives and our being will be changed forever as we discover how much and how well He loves us.

PREFACE

Over the years, after listening to stories about my life, many people have suggested that I write a book. Time after time, I laughed off the idea. It was always a struggle for me to put together enough material for a blog post or a magazine article; I could not imagine being able to write an entire book. How wrong I was.

Holding On Loosely is the evidence of how wrong I was, about my ability to write a book and so much more about life and God. My journey in tennis and life began when I left home at age 13 in search of a tennis dream programmed by my father into my mind and into the very core of my being. The mission was simply to make it.

"Making it" became an idol in my life. The closer I got to making it, the more the people who mattered to me smiled and loved me. The further I got from making it, the less of their approval I received. As life progressed, I learned very quickly that receiving love and approval was inextricably linked with being successful.

The years came and went, and I found myself the victim of the very things I had tried to control in my life. Yes, I achieved some success, but it was not the success I was told I had to achieve. Or so I assumed, as I never quite received the approval that confirmed I had reached the goal.

My life took me down paths and into situations where I never thought I would find myself. The more that success eluded me, the more I was willing to give up in order to secure it. In time I became the master manipulator of my own journey. My disease—wanting to be loved and accepted at any cost—was a common one. The symptoms were many, but none was more prevalent than my need to control my life, my relationships and my future. At one point, I would even try to control my God.

My thoughts about "making it" changed when I realized I was too old to become a successful professional tennis player. I shifted my vision to racing cars, as I came from a family involved in the sport. From there, my focus changed many times over the years. I tried business, ministry and even my early years in coaching to calm and satisfy this driving need I had within me to make it. With grit and perseverance, I experienced a degree of success on all these fronts. But in time, I became emotionally and spiritually exhausted as I was trying by my own effort to find and feel the acceptance of my father.

My relationship with God became one of entitlement and fictional codependency. I saw God in the same way I saw my natural father and all the others who had come into my life but left very quickly when they found out I wasn't quite what they thought.

In my desperation, I inevitably became a control freak and perfectionist. Outside, I portrayed the image of someone who had it all together, someone who knew God and His grace and love for people. Yet inside I continued to get further and further away from the very thing I claimed to know. My legalistic approach to God and life alienated me from the very love and life

I was looking for. I fell into the trap of *religion* and all it suppos-edly offered if I could just somehow make the grade. *Religion* cost me my life, my first marriage and many other close and valuable relationships; it led me to do the very things I con-demned others for doing.

Unfortunately, many others fall into the same trap of good intentions and self-help formulas as I did. We exhaust ourselves by the efforts we make in order to reach the destination where we believe we will finally find God. But God lives on the road of grace, where behavior and performance take a second seat to life, love and relationship. On this road, we are free to be our-selves. No more manipulations and false pretenses. No more bargaining or forcing. No more *religion* and rules. Just *Life.*

To God, the condition of our heart is what matters first. The heart is the place where Life originates. The heart is the place where everything in our lives begins. The perfect love that only God can give us is the remedy that all our hearts are seeking. Too many of us have missed this love (and continue to miss it) because we focus on our behavior, trying to be perfect.

Through this book, I pray that the eyes of your heart will be opened to see and understand that this road of grace and relationship is available to everyone, including you. God's grace does not excuse us to live as degenerates, but instead it helps us to understand that we cannot "make it" by our own efforts. Trying to do so will not result in changing our behavior; it will only result in getting to the end of this life's road and finding we have missed it.

I began to realize this truth inside a metal tube at 35,000 feet above the earth. It was on this flight, in the midst of my career as a tennis coach to some of the best female players on the planet, that I finally surrendered and ceased my own efforts. What followed from that moment is the story in these pages. You will be able to look down the path into the series of events that led me to learn and understand that the only way to meet the *real* God, and not the one that *religion* speaks of, is by letting go and holding on loosely. I learned this as I coached players to reach the place we know in sports as "the Zone." During my journey, God revealed to me through various means, including Scripture, that the Zone was where we are all meant to live.

Due to the nature of my coaching work with professional players, I have chosen in this book to conceal their identities for their protection. In the chapters that follow, "Stacey" is the name I have given a character who represents a combination of four players and others I have had the privilege to work with during my time as a professional coach. "Terry" also represents a combination of several people who came alongside me at points in my journey and helped me understand how to find and invite into my heart the very things that we are all ulti-mately looking for. They were individuals God invited to share with me the next piece of the puzzle.

The events in this book are those that impacted me most in my journey. I have done my best to recount them in an order that reflects how and when God led me, though they are not necessarily told in perfect chronological order and some of them combined together to show the complete lessons I was taught by God. As you read this story God has led me to tell, I hope you will come into the same place as I have.

I have learned that in spite of my many flaws, I am still loved and accepted. Where I thought I would meet shame, condemnation and disappointment from an angry father tired of seeing me fail and fall short, I have found it is the safest place for me when I am at my worst. You see, I have finally begun to discover that the outcome of my life and endeavors are in God's hands, and they will continue to change me from one degree of glory to another as I get to know and understand how much He truly loves me.

As you read the pages of this book, I pray that you will find, as I have, that God is for you, He has been all along, and He will continue to be always!

CHAPTER 1

RELIGION

Instead of bread I get groans for my supper,
then leave the table and vomit my anguish.
The worst of my fears has come true,
what I've dreaded most has happened.
My repose is shattered, my peace destroyed.
No rest for me, ever—death has invaded life.

—Job 3:25–26

Yes, Lord. I am not doing enough.

I say it to myself as I finish reading my daily Scripture.

Please forgive me for not doing enough and not working hard enough. That's why I am not getting the blessing I want in my life.

As I finish this silent prayer, I know deep inside that something is not right. Yet time is passing, and I need to get ready for this morning's practice. Slapping my face, I tell myself to wake up and stop daydreaming. After all, God only helps those who help themselves, right? Though I've never found this verse in the Bible, I convince myself, *Yes, that's right.*

It is a cold winter morning, and fog is covering the field next to the hotel. We are about to begin another training session, and I have told my player this will get her closer to that coveted prize she so longs for.

"Good morning, Stacey."

"Good morning, Pablo."

"Sleep well?"

"Only two hours as I am so jet-lagged."

"I know what you mean. That flight was really long. Still, forget the 12-hour time difference and the long flight. We have to work! Life doesn't wait for anyone," I reply. "Come on, let's go!"

As we start to run, I notice that Stacey is just not up for it this morning. My common sense tells me it would be better to postpone this until later, but my no-pain-no-gain attitude kicks in immediately. With a great big, "Come on!" I wake up Stacey (as well as the entire hotel, I suspect). By the time we come to the end of the run, both Stacey and I are alive again. We stretch, then we head for our rooms to shower before breakfast.

I enter the elevator as a few players, long in the tooth, walk out and ignore my "Good morning." I suspect their faces are the consequence of hearing my zealous early-morning session outside with Stacey. As I enter my room, I think to myself, *Yes, this is what it's all about, working hard to get the most out of life.*

Getting out of the shower, I can't help but notice that the feeling I went in with is slowly dissipating. Once again I find myself looking for the next fix, the next training session, the next schedule of matches, the next, the next, the next....

When I meet Stacey in the restaurant, she seems, awake and happy, so perhaps I am the only one losing vision and focus. We have breakfast together, then head for the courts.

Soon after entering the court and beginning practice, I notice the same dejected look on Stacey's face that she had when we met for the morning run. The more instruction I give her, the more dejected she becomes. On instruction number 1,020, she finally turns around, throws the racquet against the fence and shouts "Stop!" At first, I think she is injured, so I rush over to where she is sitting on the court crying. I ask her what is wrong, but she does not respond. I ask again and again and get no response.

Suddenly she answers, "Nothing I ever do is good enough. I always need to do better. Will I ever get there? Will I ever reach a place where I can rest and stop trying harder all the time?"

In her outburst I see real anger, the kind of anger built up through years of frustration. As always, I dismiss her excuses and tell her to toughen up and get on with it. "The weak never make it," I say. "We have to sacrifice if we want to make it and accomplish what the few privileged ones experience in their lives and careers." Yet my words are hollow as I know the same anger is inside me. I have been carrying it for a long time, and it shows up every time I don't get my way or when God does not deliver into my lap the results or blessing I expect. It erupts at the hotel registration desk when I don't get the room I wanted, and it seems to get worse the more I try to control it.

Composing herself on the outside, Stacey gets up and we continue practice. When we finish, she leaves the court looking dead again. *I wonder why,* I think to myself. *Her tennis got better toward the end of practice, so why is she looking so dejected? After all, that famous coach passing by our court commented on how good her forehand was looking.*

The day finishes, and the tournament does for us also as Stacey loses the first round. The loss only helps cement my conviction that we are not doing enough, despite the long and arduous days on the court and in the gym. *Somehow we need to work harder so we can get the results we are looking for,* I think to myself.

After what seems like an eternity, we reach the airport to travel to our next destination. I get out of the car first to unload the bags, as most tournament drivers don't bother to help with this chore, and we don't seem to have an exception today. While I do this, Stacey is looking for two trolleys for our baggage. I notice she is arguing with some guy over one of the trolleys. As I approach the situation, I hear the guy telling her to take a hike.

"Excuse me!" I say, trying to keep my cool. After we exchange a few pleasantries, I conquer the trolley and we move inside the terminal, where we are met by possibly the longest line in airline history. As we join the end of the line, I wonder if we are now waiting at a different airport than the one where we originally arrived. I am doing my best to calm down from my confrontation with the trolley bandit earlier when I notice that a group of kids is being allowed to jump to the front. This does not do anything to ease my anger and lack of patience, so I follow my instinct with a very sarcastic shout, "Oh yeah, that's a classic!" A few people around me smile, but as usual I am the only one to say something.

After a 45-minute wait, we reach the front of the line. On my way to the counter, I tell myself that I will be calm and radiate the love and grace of Jesus. It works until the lady behind the counter informs me with the most nagging voice I have ever heard that my bag is two kilos over the weight limit and I will have to pay extra if I want to travel today. Suddenly the idea of letting Jesus shine through me disappears and the same anger I saw on Stacey's face earlier erupts from within me.

I unload the frustrations of dealing with the trolley, seeing a group of kids jump the line, and waiting for 45 minutes. That's not to mention all the frustration that has been lurking inside me for quite a while because I have been too busy to deal with it. I've been focusing all my efforts on pretending the frustrations are not there in the first place. By the time I finish my rant, everyone in that section of the airport is looking at me—including the coach with whom I was sharing Jesus yesterday. His face is lifeless as he looks on in disbelief. Our eyes meet for a brief second, and sudden guilt and condemnation overwhelm me.

As I walk away I can't believe what has just happened. Outside I continue to try justifying myself, yet inside I feel totally lost. *Not only did I blow my witness with the other coach, but where did all the good intention to do the right thing go? How could I lose control in such a way?*

In the meantime Stacey has been watching all of this quietly. Little do I know she is absorbing and succumbing to the disease that is slowly and surely eating me up inside.

Sitting in the airport terminal, I look straight out the window where rows of planes are parked at the gates. My gaze firmly fixed on the horizon as the sun sets, I wonder where God is and where that initial joy and freedom I felt when I met Him well over a decade ago has gone. *Surely the answer is here outside myself somewhere. I just need to look harder to find it,* I think to myself.

Just as I am beginning to fall asleep, worn out by all that has gone on and the emotional weight I have been carrying, I notice a newspaper out of the corner of my eye. There's a picture of the preacher whose book about the seven keys to a successful life I recently read. I pick up the paper and begin to read the article. It describes how readers can experience success and fulfillment in their lives if they just follow the seven simple steps given in the book. My heart is directing me to the sports section to see what has been going on, but that little religious voice inside me is pushing self-maintenance, the need to put together the example-to-all-society Pablo once again. I try desperately to fight it but to no avail. My mind tells me I am fighting God and, even in my blind state, I know that's a battle I won't win. Surely God is not interested in the sports results but only in driving me to perfection, which is what pleases Him in my view.

So I put down the newspaper and begin to beat myself up once again: *See Pablo, there is the answer. You are not being perfect enough with these seven steps. You need to do more.* The problem is I don't know where this *more* is going to come from, as by now I have exhausted all my self-effort, all my striving, all my putting and holding things together in my life. And not only in my life; I have been also trying to hold things together in the lives of others, as Jesus said we must put others before ourselves. *Oh this Jesus, He must have been amazing to be able to perform perfectly every single day of His life.*

When our flight is called, I leave the newspaper behind. I walk to the plane wondering where God is. Yes, the newspaper reminded me about the seven steps, and many would say God was speaking to me through it. Yes, I know it's all up to me now as He has done His part. So why do I feel so empty? Why do I feel that the harder I try, the further I fall away—and, worse yet, the further Stacey seems to be from getting to where she needs to be?

On the plane I open my notebook and title seven pages, each page with one of the seven steps the preacher taught. I set some goals for how I am going to apply each of these steps, and by the end of this exercise I feel good about myself again.

I am sure God does too, as He can see I am back on my way with my energies focused on these steps He inspired the preacher to teach to help no-good, failing saints, or maybe sinners, like me. This good feeling gives me enough confidence to approach God again and ask forgiveness for my Oscar-winning performance at the check-in counter earlier in the day.

The captain announces over the loudspeaker that we have reached cruising altitude and our flight will be a smooth one all the way. As I tilt my seat back I think to myself, *You see, there it is. The blessing of God has returned because I am on the right track again after praying and planning my steps. He must be very pleased with me.*

I turn to Stacey and tell her that we are going to have a great tournament coming up. "I can just feel it," I say to her.

She smiles back at me. I see both hope and despair in her face. Hope because she trusts what I say, but also despair because she knows deep inside, as I do, that this good feeling will last only until the next obstacle arrives in our path.

After setting up camp at our next hotel, we go down to the club for practice, which goes extremely well. We are both very hopeful about tomorrow's match as Stacey has played and defeated this opponent twice before. I feel I am making good progress with the seven-steps formula, so God must have something good for us tomorrow.

On match day, Stacey kills her opponent with a convincing 6–1, 6–1 victory. On our way to the gym after the match, we get more good news from the main scoreboard: the seeded player on our part of the draw has just retired from her match. *Yes! You see, I knew it! God is with us again and He is blessing us. This is our tournament,* I think to myself.

Stacey goes on to win the next two matches, and we now find ourselves in the semifinals against an opponent we both know she can defeat. As we sit down for dinner, I notice that look of despair on Stacey's face once again. I can't believe it. *Where did this come from? We are having such a good run, and she is feeling uncertain now?*

I dive into her, trying to fix the situation. With one of my best pep talks, I try with all my might to force the change in her behavior and mindset that will be crucial for a win tomorrow. I can see it is not working, so I excuse myself to my room, where I rush through my notes on the seven steps. *What am I missing, and why this is happening?* I pray quickly, but as usual I can't hear anything when I most need God to say something. Maybe He is angry again and has withdrawn His blessing. *What have I done wrong in the last 24 hours that is causing me to fall out of favor with God?*

I return to the table where I left Stacey and find her talking with another player and coach. She looks happy and calm; maybe God has answered my prayer. I wait for them to finish the conversation, and as soon as the visitors leave, Stacey's face falls again—proving my theory wrong.

Heading back to my room after dinner, I realize inside me that something is not right. With every passing minute, tomorrow seems to be slipping out of our grasp. *God, why?* I ask. *Why does this always happen when we are on the brink? Why do You play games with us? Here I am tithing, praying and even following the seven steps, and things don't go where we need them to go. Why God, why?*

At breakfast the next day, I see that Stacey's despair has turned into fear. I ask her a number of questions in hopes of distracting her, but nothing I can say is going to make this fear go away. It has dug a very big trench in her mind, and it is not going to leave anytime soon.

I sit and watch the match as I do so many times, bargaining with God. I find myself playing superstitious games in my mind, yet nothing seems to work.

Stacey loses the match in three sets. I am very angry and frustrated at Stacey, but more so at God. He is such a hard guy to please, and He just loves to play games with us. His favorite seems to be dangling the carrot in front of our faces. Yep, He must really like that one. In my life, He always seems to take the carrot away just as I am getting out the salt and pepper, ready to eat it.

I feel totally numb as I look at my notebook. By now I am overcome with guilt because of my angry reaction to God, and I can forget praying or even thinking about Him. He must be fuming by now. I close my eyes on the way back to the hotel and try to pray, but as I suspected, the heavenly firewall is up again and God is nowhere to be found...at least that is what I feel.

Back in my room I fall into bed in a complete daze, wondering what this is all about. I have been in this gig well over a decade by now, and by now it is obvious that I am tired, very tired. I begin to wonder if there is any truth to this whole God thing when my phone rings. It's a friend who runs a church. In my desperation to find answers and return to that good feeling and most importantly the blessing, I spill my guts to him. He hears me out and asks if there is any sin I might be involved in to cause things to be going this way. Many things come to mind, most of which I can't mention as they are too embarrassing. What would he think of me if he found out; and, worse yet, what if God heard me say them? Clearly God knows my sins, and I know He knows, but the pretending game has a very clever way of engulfing our minds and allowing us to live in fantasyland.

My friend closes the call, advising me to spend more time with God and fast if I have a chance so I might be able to hear God. He recommends I read a book that has just come out in order not to miss what God has for me. I thank him for the call.

I immediately turn on my laptop and search for the book online. I find that it is being sold in a bookshop just down the road from the hotel. It is late and I am very tired, but shops in this town are open late. I think this book might be the answer to getting God back on my side. So I must make the effort and run down to the shop—in spite of the pouring rain outside. *This rain is from the Devil,* I think to myself. *He is just trying to stop me from getting God back on my side!* I'm more determined than ever to get the book.

Running, I get to the shop just before it closes. When the store clerk tells me I am buying the last copy she has, that great feeling I've been missing so badly comes back. The firewall has been turned off, and the blessings return. *Thank you, God, that even when I am unfaithful you are still with me,* I say silently.

I run back to the hotel, and by now I am sneezing pretty badly. *Oh well,* I think. *It's a small price to pay for this beauty of a book.*

I stay awake long enough to read about half the book, then I dare to whisper a prayer. Yes, it feels good. I think it got through to God.

The next day I am feeling sick, but I decide I must fast as this is what my friend advised. God is not One to wait around for compliance, so I must keep Him happy. Stacey calls to see why I am not in the lobby for breakfast. I tell her I am not hungry this morning, to go ahead without me, and that I will meet her at 11 o'clock at the airport shuttle.

On the way to the airport, I try to focus on the questions Stacey is asking. But I am becoming very weak as I am sick and have not eaten anything. I force myself together and ask God for strength as I believe this sacrifice will get me closer to Him and His blessing.

When we reach our next destination, a driver in a very nice car meets us and drives us to a very nice hotel. Stacey's room at the hotel is ready, but mine isn't. By now I am nearly dead and I have no room! I assure Stacey that I am happy to wait. Though rage erupts inside me, I am too weak to fight so I conk out on a sofa in the lounge.

Three hours later the receptionist wakes me and gives me the key to my room. By the time I get into the room, I am breaking out in a cold sweat and shaking uncontrollably. The bag of peanuts on top of the TV is calling my name. Eventually I just can't take it anymore and devour the contents in three seconds.

Immediately the thought enters my mind: *Jesus spent 40 days in the desert without food and you cannot even manage a single day?* Feeling terribly guilty, I repent for eating the peanuts and pass out in the bed, hoping God is not too upset.

I wake up the next morning realizing we have the day off. Staying in bed, I start to feel guilty by 10 a.m., believing I should be praying and reading my new book. I try to engage myself but realize there is just no way it is going to happen. I begin to think this God of mine likes to play hard to get. He doesn't engage when we engage; He engages when He wants, and since He is God we just have to hope for the best. To be honest, I begin thinking maybe He is schizophrenic and what He is feeling on a particular day is unpredictable. It seems His mood swings according to what I do or don't do; I feel His presence at the times when I behave the most perfectly, and at the times when I don't He is just not there.

Will this merry-go-round ever stop? Will I ever get to that place some speak of where I am able to be myself? I guess those people who are okay to be themselves have reached perfection. Me? Well, I've got a long way to go. I feel like a total failure inside, though outside everyone thinks I am a winner as I am always "doing great." I appear to be so together, yet inside it's a different story.

I pick up my seven-steps book, my notes, my Bible and my newest book to start studying. They seem like three-ton bricks, yet it's up to me to carry them and learn from them. Then maybe I will reach that place where I will be okay. If I can only get there, I believe Stacey and her tennis will be okay too. But will it? *Of course it will,* I reassure myself. After all, God loves me. At least, that is what the books tell me, right? It would be nice to know and feel that love more often. If only it was possible to experience His love without having to do all this stuff.

I will soon find out how wrong I am.

CHAPTER 2

LOOSENING THE GRIP

Dear God,
I am so afraid to open my clenched fists!
Who will I be when I have nothing left to hold on to?
Who will I be when I stand before you with empty hands?
Please help me to gradually open my hands
and to discover that I am not what I own,
but what you want to give me.
And what you want to give me is love,
unconditional, everlasting love.
Amen.

—Henri Nouwen

Stacey reaches the quarterfinals in our current tournament before being defeated, then once again we are back on the road to our next event. Though I'm still somewhat sick from not eating a few days ago, I am regaining my resolve to find that perfect place in life. Little do I know that the flight I'm about to board will be unlike any I've ever taken.

It begins just like all the other flights, but it changes when I look out the window, stare into the horizon and cry out silently to God. Asking Him what is so wrong in my life, I begin to cry like a child. I ask Him why I am so dry, so empty, so lonely and so lost. I tell Him that He feels just like my dad— never happy, never pleased unless I am perfect all the time at everything I do. I tell Him I want to give up the never-ending striving and just be myself, that I want desperately to stop wearing this mask of good intentions. I just want to be loved and to be able to love as Jesus did, and I want to be *real* and stop pretending. *God, if You can hear me and You are different than I think You are, please show me why all this is happening to me.*

The tears flow as they have not done in all of my adult life. After I stop crying, I go to the airplane's restroom to wash my face. That's when I notice a quietness and stillness in my spirit. I feel at rest for the first time in well over a decade. It feels like time is standing still and that maybe, just maybe, God has heard my cries. Everything inside me is desperate to believe God is not the heavenly policeman and drill sergeant I have imagined, but that He is the loving, compassionate and fun Father whom Jesus talked about in the Gospels. Though few of my friends seem to know this kind of Father, I am hopeful He is real.

As our plane lands, the pilot informs us we will be waiting on the tarmac for a bit as there is no gate currently available for us. Normally I would be in no mood to hang out, but I am not greatly bothered by this delay. It's a good thing, since I don't have any choice but to wait it out.

The "wait for a bit" turns out to be 45 minutes, yet I am surprisingly calm and at peace. When we reach the baggage area in the airport terminal, Stacey spots a juggler.

"Look, Pablo," she says.

Now, juggling is very familiar to tennis coaches as it is something we use to help children develop their coordination, dexterity and motor skills. I have always loved juggling, but regrettably I have never been able to progress past the standard three-ball routine. Naturally I am attracted to someone who can juggle more than three objects at a time as I appreciate the skill involved.

"Let's go have a look at this guy," I tell Stacey after we pick up our bags.

As we approach him, I notice he is juggling four objects. His taskmaster/trainer is throwing in another object every time he sees fit. While we stand there, the juggler moves from handling four objects to handling seven. As the number of objects he juggles increases, so does the crowd and the clink of coins dropping into the hat on the ground beside him. I notice the juggler is becoming tired, but, in a language I can't understand, the task-master is obviously telling him to keep going. The crowd continues to throw coins in the hat; now is not the time to stop.

We stand there looking on in amazement until the exhausted juggler suddenly stops and all the objects fall to the ground. Though the trainer is smiling, I can see fear in the juggler's eyes, fear of letting the trainer down. The master/trainer turns around and greets the crowd with a great big smile and thank-you.

While everyone is clapping and cheering, I have another time-stands-still moment. Right there in the baggage area, everything seems to become quiet around me. And for the first time in more than 13 years, I hear a voice in my heart. "That's why you feel the way you do," the voice says as I look at the juggler and the dropped objects scattered on the ground.

The voice is so clear; I have not heard a voice like it in years. I feel an amazing peace. My mind is still, yet my heart is doing summersaults with excitement.

Stacey tells me the driver from the tournament is waiting for us, but I don't want to leave this place. *Could this be God? I ask myself. Could this be Him answering my prayer from the plane? Could this really be happening?*

Forcing myself to move on and into the waiting car, I feel desperate to get to the hotel. When we arrive, I check in, tell Stacey I will see her in a few hours for practice and rush to my room. I feel like this incident in the airport was a dream. I want to know more, and I want to know what the voice meant by, *that's why you feel the way you do.* I want to know if this is really God or if it is the Devil tricking me again.

I start praying, hoping I can get the voice to speak to me once more. Nothing happens. But I am so excited that I can hardly sit down. I unpack my bags as quickly as I can and jump into the shower. I am amazed at the joy and freedom I feel even though I haven't opened my Bible all day. I feel so good inside, you'd think the voice had told me we were going to win a Grand Slam or that a million bucks was coming my way.

I call Stacey's room, and we arrange to meet downstairs in half an hour to go to the courts for practice. As I hang up the phone, I remind myself that I need to hear this voice again. I wish it would whisper again to my heart, but I hear nothing. I open my Bible and read a bit to be sure I have done my duty.

As we get into the courtesy car for the trip to the courts, Stacey asks, "What's happened to you?"

It seems like a strange question to me. "Why do you ask?" I reply.

"Well, have you had a look at your face lately?" she asks.

"I guess I haven't."

"Well, you should. The last time I saw that look on your face was when I won my last tournament."

Her words go right through me, as her last win had been nearly a year earlier.

I quickly laugh off her remark. But inside, I realize I've only been happy when I've had results, when I've achieved my goals, when I've felt like I have been very good. I think back on this morning's occurrence and, though all I did was cry and feel like giving up, the experience itself is making me happy. I feel so good inside.

We arrive at the club, and I am greeted by the tournament director and a few of the volunteers to whom I have grown close over the years of participating in their event. I spend a few minutes with a journalist who asks me if the last tournament is a sign that things are beginning to turn around for Stacey. I respond that this is my hope. Inside I am desperately longing for the turnaround to happen not only for her game, but in my own life, for everything inside me, for my own heart.

On the practice court, Stacey and I spend half our time slot watching her opponent argue with her coach. As I take this in, I can't help but remember this morning's experience in the airport. The words I heard keep revolving in my mind. *Who was it?* I ask myself, *and what did it mean?*

When our practice time on the court is up, Stacey and I venture on to the gym. While working out together, Stacey tells me how much she enjoyed practice today and how great it was to have me with her on the court.

"What do you mean?" I ask.

"You were so relaxed and positive, and the best part is that you said so little but it was all good and helped me so much," she responds.

I happen to be standing in front of a huge mirror as she

says this, and I can't help but look at my reflection and wonder what the heck is going on.

After we finish in the gym, I go down to the referee's office to have a look at the draw. We play tomorrow, and the first match is a good one.

Later that night back at the hotel, I am checking my emails and find a link someone has sent me to download the movie *Facing the Giants*. The title appeals to me, so I click the link. As I wait for the movie to download, I thank God again for the day and look back at the book with those seven steps for success.

Which of these steps did I clearly fulfill in a masterful way during that flight? It must have been a good one that led to my wonderful experience in the plane and the airport terminal.

I scan through all of the steps, but none of them seem to relate to what has happened. This concerns me as it leads me to think this incident may have been caused by the Enemy. *After all, I have not had any real control over what has happened so far today. Yes, the occurrences have brought amazing change to me and Stacey, but where is God in all of this? Why is He not quoting Scripture to me or correcting me like I've always thought He has done in the past?*

As I'm going down this desperate road in my mind, the computer beeps indicating the download is finished. *I love these nice hotels. The Internet is just so fast,* I think to myself.

I open the movie and hit play, promising myself I will only watch some of it as it is getting late and we have an early start tomorrow. For those of you who have not seen the movie, it is about a high school football coach who is a believer, but nothing is working in his life. His team is losing; he and his wife are unable to have children; and his attempts at trying to control things only seem to make matters worse. Behind his back, a group of parents arrange a meeting with his assistant coach to discuss getting rid of him. He discovers the meeting and hears what is said.

Up to this point, the movie is like any other to me. It is good and I am enjoying it, but it is nearly midnight, so I decide I will finish watching it tomorrow. Suddenly, I hear the voice that spoke to my heart in the airport terminal.

"Wait."

Oh my gosh, I think. *There it is again. I have not prayed or meditated for at least half an hour. I have not done anything spiritual, I am just watching a movie, and—like the song—"boom, there it is."*

I sit up on my bed and turn up the volume on my laptop. Sure enough, the movie takes an amazing, sudden turn. The coach finds out he is responsible for the infertility in his marriage, and he finally gives up. He actually breaks down in a similar way to my in-flight incident, then he spends the night reading and praying. The way this scene is speaking to my heart really catches my attention. Tears begin to roll down my cheeks, and I hear the voice say, "You have to let go, Pablo."

Immediately I take out my notebook and pen. *What do I let go of?* I ask.

"Everything," I hear in response.

Everything?

"Yes, everything."

Sitting there for what seems like an eternity, I feel numb and as though there are two of me. I desperately want this to be God. I want so much for Him to be behind all that is happening.

I start trying to plan how I am going to let go of everything when the voice says, "You are juggling again, Pablo."

What do you mean? I ask, but there is no response. I wait a while longer and even catch myself trying to reproduce the same voice within me. It ends up sounding like a religious monkey.

I am wide awake, as you can imagine, so I stop planning things out and go back to the movie. An older man who prays over the student lockers every day comes into the coach's office and shares a word he believes is from God. The word is based on Scriptures that speak of staying where God has opened a door and waiting for God to bring a harvest for His glory. The coach continues with his life as usual after this, but things begin to change for him. Someone buys him a new car. He and his wife start a family. The high school team wins the state championship. Revival breaks out at the school.

The movie ends and I sit there on my bed, wondering what is going on. Whatever it is, I'm amazed. I have not felt this good in years. I feel close to something or someone, but I still don't realize it is God. My recognition is blocked by the religion and the need to please that are still inside me. I feel like I am losing control of my life, but I am not worried. Deep down I am very skeptical as no one has ever shown me or spoken about God being this way. Yes, many have said He is my spiritual Father and He loves me, but I have never felt His love. In fact, apart from when I first became a Christian, I have always believed I had to do something for Him after all He did for me.

The alarm goes off. It is 6 a.m., and it is match day. Stacey plays the first match, so we need to warm up early to be ready.

Every part of me wants to be sure I don't do anything to upset whatever will keep this voice happy. I want to keep hearing what it has to say. I have just had the most remarkable day of my life since making the decision to accept Jesus. It has been over a decade of many long, dry, lonely years that have worn me down and produced nothing but anger and frustration in me. Yesterday was an absolute beauty, and I must be sure there are more days like that.

I take a few minutes to pray and read my Bible, but I hear nothing. Yet I feel so great. *This short time with God must have been pleasing to Him,* I think to myself.

Going through my morning routine, I am very relaxed. This peace stays with me throughout the first part of the day. Stacey wins her match comfortably. All is well.

When a fellow coach invites me to join a group getting together for a beer later in the day, I decline his invitation—something inside is compelling me to stay in and pray to be sure all continues to be well. Since we don't have a match tomorrow, I tell Stacey we will practice only once tomorrow, in the afternoon, as she is playing well and had a great match today.

"Pablo, are you okay?" she asks me.

"Yes. Why do you keep asking me that?" I reply.

"This will be the first day in more than a year you are letting me practice just once."

I laugh, but at the same time I wonder if that is really true. I try to recall the last day we practiced only once, and I can't remember. So I assume Stacey is right.

Trying to save face, I tell her I must be having a blonde moment and to make the most of the opportunity as it won't last. She laughs.

I think back over the day, recollecting every moment to determine if I had done anything wrong. You see, inside I am still performing, still juggling. Little do I know that the good place I am in has nothing to do with what I did or didn't do. I am at this place because I have been invited here by the Owner—who actually likes me. And I would find out later it was the Owner's voice I had been hearing.

Heading back to the hotel, Stacey and I board the van transporting players and coaches. It's operating at full capacity this trip, and I have no choice but to sit next to a coach I really don't like. I've had several run-ins with him, and I find him very hard to love. With my mind firmly focused on being good, I sit down next to him and smile. I can see from the look on his face that this surprises him, which makes me feel great inside.

Another coach with whom he is a friend approaches and greets him. My nemesis replies to his friend in a very loud and sarcastic voice, "I am great, especially with the company I have next to me." They both laugh, triggering something inside me. I look at him and tell him he is an absolute loser and that people like him are the very reason condoms are made. The argument escalates to the point that other passengers ask us to calm down and relax. I get up and move to the back of the van where I stand for the rest of the trip.

With every passing moment my anger increases. I really want to smack this guy. When we finally get back to the hotel, I go straight to my room. By now all the good feelings have vanished. I berate myself, as I realize that in my anger I went too far. I try to pray and repent. I plead with God, but the more I plead the worse I feel. *I have blown it again.*

Hoping to feel a bit better about what happened, I call a friend to talk. It's no help. So I try to think of something I can do to make amends for my actions so God will be happy and I can feel good again. Nothing comes to mind.

Dinner with Stacey is a temporary distraction. As we return to our rooms, I am beginning to think we should train twice tomorrow after all. I call the club, but there are no courts available. So I tell Stacey we will go to the gym.

"I guess the honeymoon is over, hey Pablo?" she says.

"Yes, I guess it is," I reply. "See you in the morning. Good night."

As I close my room door behind me, I feel gutted and empty once again. *Where have those positive feelings from the last two days gone? Why couldn't I just keep my mouth shut in the bus? Why, why, why?*

I hit the bed and fall asleep. During the night, I dream that I am back at the airport watching the juggler. There is no one with me except the juggler and the master. And unlike the real-life incident in the airport terminal, this juggler has more than ten objects in the air. At the same time, his eyes are firmly fixed on the master who is encouraging him. I can't help but notice the love in the master's tone of voice as he talks to the juggler.

Suddenly the juggler drops the objects. The master rushes over, embraces him and tells him he is doing great. He helps the juggler pick up the objects, and together they begin to try again. This happens repeatedly, and the more it happens the more objects the juggler handles looking relaxed and happy.

As I am noticing this, the master turns to me with a huge smile and asks if I want to try. I jump in without hesitation, but tell him I am not very good. Reassuring me, he says, "Just let go and see how you do."

I am desperate to impress the master; I start with three objects but keep dropping them. Every time I drop them, I apologize and promise to do better next time. This happens repeatedly, and in my anxiety I completely forget the master is there. With each passing try, I exhaust myself more and more. After what seems an eternity, I stop. I am down to one object, and I am dizzy from picking up all the objects I've dropped. I'm mentally exhausted.

I glance up to find the master looking at me with the most radiant and loving face I have ever seen in my life. I feel so bad that I have failed, and all I can do is apologize. I start crying, telling him I will work harder so he can be proud of me as he was the other juggler.

Speaking of the other juggler, he seems to have disappeared. I don't see him anywhere. The master comes over to me and kneels down to my level. He sits there beside me and says nothing. I hide my face in my hands, looking down at the ground. He must think I am such a failure,

"That thought is often in your head, isn't it?" the master says, laughing kindly.

I look up at him. "You can read my thoughts?" I ask.

"Pablo, I can do so much more than that," he replies. "Get up, let's try again."

"I am so tired, master. I'm sorry, I just can't."

"I know," he says. "In fact you are not only tired now, but this is how you feel in your life every day, isn't it?"

Crying again, I answer him by nodding my head.

"Yes, it is very hard when you try to do it all in your own strength. It seems that the harder you try, the harder it gets. Just like the juggling. You know something?" he asks. "If you never got past one ball, I would still love you. In fact, if you never juggled again, I would still love you and would be as proud of you as if you were able to juggle 10 objects."

At that moment, I feel a bolt of love go through me with such intensity that it knocks me to the ground. As I lie there,

I look up at the master who is watching me. I feel so loved and so welcome, so full and so complete.

"You see Pablo, you have to let go of all you have thought wrongly about Me, the idea that I am a horrible Master who punishes you every time you fail. You have to let go of that angry God you have been serving, the One for whom you are forcing yourself to pray and read your Bible. Give up all your efforts to try so desperately to please Me, and quit this mission you are on to earn My love. Will you let Me show you who I am, how much I love you and how much you mean to Me?"

With this last word, I suddenly recognize this as the same voice I heard at the airport.

I quickly return to my feet and ask the Master, "Are you God?" He smiles as he picks up the balls I had dropped.

"Remember the juggler I was working with before you?"

"Yes," I reply.

"That was you; that's why you couldn't find him."

"But I can't even juggle one object," I remind Him.

"Yes that's right, but I can help you with that and so much more if you just let go and trust Me. Trust what I tell you and show you."

I rush over to Him, hug Him and tell Him I love Him so much. I thank Him again and again, and before I know it I am awake.

CHAPTER 3

THE ZONE

I came so they can have real and eternal life, more and better life than they ever dreamed of.

—John 10:10

What has just happened? I think as I lie in the bed wide awake.

I've woken up from nightmares breathing very fast and scared, but this morning I am feeling very still. It's almost like I've taken a one-milligram Xanax, but with the huge difference that I don't feel weak or unable to function. I feel totally energized yet strangely still and at peace. The joy within me is out of this world, and though I could scream like a madman I choose to lie here and enjoy the moment.

As you can imagine, every part of me wants to stay in bed and enjoy this peaceful state. I stare through the window at the beautiful view. Everything seems so perfect, so still, so right. I feel like I am in touch with something far greater and bigger than I have ever experienced. For the first time in all my years, I feel loved, but most importantly, I feel approved. It's a weird feeling—like I am loved for who I am and not for what I have done or can do for anyone. It feels as though I could retire and do nothing else for the rest of my life and still be approved of and loved.

This place feels similar to the place we know and call the Zone in sports. According to the scientific community, the Zone is a place where you flow; it's the result of completely focused motivation. It is a single-minded immersion, representing the ultimate in harnessing the emotions in the service of performing and learning.

In this flow of the Zone, the emotions are contained and channeled, but moving beyond that they are positive, energized and aligned with the task at hand. The ennui of depression or the agitation of anxiety will interrupt it.

A feeling of spontaneous joy, even rapture, while performing a task is the hallmark of flow. In its extreme state, time slows down and unusually high physical performance may be achieved.

Wow, that's a mouthful! I just know I feel great right now, and I want to stay here. As a coach, I know the Zone is very real and can be achieved in a sporting activity. It is the place where we touch something beyond ourselves and our ordinary mindset. Most athletes and coaches know the Zone is a very common thing, but could this be also possible in my walk and daily relationship with God?

Could this describe the place where Jesus lived?

Could my meeting with God in the dream have led me to a place similar to the Zone?

Could this be the place where He meant all of us to live? I wonder.

Could this be the place within us that we inhabit when we discover we are loved by our Father in Heaven and know it as clearly as Jesus knew it?

I have so many questions, yet I am not about to let them spoil this place I have been invited into.

While the feelings inside me are the same I've experienced in the Zone, there is something very different here. I didn't go through any routine like most athletes do in order to get here; I just woke up in this reality. I haven't done anything to deserve or help to produce this feeling—which for me is huge. *I have to investigate this further. Where in the Bible is there evidence of this?*

What I am about to find out will totally change my life and the way I understand my relationship with God. I clearly do not want to get religious about this, but this newfound freedom is far too good to pass up. I need to find out more about it, as a small part of me thinks the enemy of my heart could be misleading me. Somehow this seems too mystical, mysterious and fun to be from God. On the other hand, I think, it might be the result of being one with God as Jesus was. *Could this be the reality we are each supposed to live in when our lives are fully surrendered to Him?*

The phone rings. It's Stacey.

"Hi, Pablo. How are you?" she asks.

"I am fine, thanks. How did you sleep?"

"I slept really well. You know, I am feeling so good it's amazing. Ever since you started to calm down and relax and be happier, it's rubbing off on me. Somehow I am changed too," she confesses.

"Wow, that's pretty amazing, hey?" I exclaim.

"Yes, it is. Lately I am feeling as though you like me and you really want the best for me. And I feel like your desire is sincere. It's not just because you want to look good as a coach."

Her words trigger a time-stands-still moment, and the truth from Scripture, *The world will know you because of your love for one another,* flashes into my mind.

The two of us speak a bit more about the day's practice plans and agree on a time to meet downstairs.

I am so excited I start shouting and jumping on my bed like a child. I jump so enthusiastically that one of the legs on the bed breaks. I can feel the presence of Someone else in the room with me; an amazing warmth pervades the room. But I don't stop. I continue to dance and jump. It's almost as if I have entered the twilight zone.

I know I am not alone anymore and, as I come down from my euphoria, I drop down to my knees and begin to cry. I have never cried as often as I am lately. *What is this? What is happening to me?* I wonder. I feel so together, so whole, so positive, so still and in the moment. With each passing moment, I care less and less about yesterday and, for sure, I could not give a monkey's tonsil about tomorrow. *Jesus, this is what You meant about not worrying about tomorrow?*

Oh Father, I sigh, as I weep again. *This is really You, isn't it?*

"Yes it is, Juan Pablo," He replies, using my whole name rather than the westernized shorter version of it. No one has called me by my full name in years. I realize He does this to show me that He knows me better and knows much more about me than I think. His voice speaking my name sends healing waves through me.

Frequently on these trips I have thought how nice it would be to have someone accompanying me, but right now I am happy for the time alone with God. There is no one else in this room but Him and me, loving and enjoying each other freely. A Father and a son have reunited today. The image of the prodigal son in Scripture flashes into my mind, and I realize I have finally returned home to my Daddy in Heaven!

Meeting Stacey for breakfast, she can see I have been crying. It doesn't matter how much I washed my face the tears I've cried are obvious. Despite noticing Stacey doesn't say anything. She's probably too scared to ask what happened.

"Oh, it's so great to be here, isn't it Stacey?" I blurt out.

"Yes, Pablo, it really is. There is a real peace about this place," she says.

I smile within me, as I know this peace has nothing to do with the place. The Prince of Peace has joined us for breakfast this morning. And though Stacey and I can't see Him, I know He is there as He promised He would be.

I could stay here having breakfast all day. I don't feel any of my past desire to rush off to the courts and get started with the tournament. But we have a schedule to keep, so we move on to catch the bus.

As we arrive at the stadium, a journalist approaches and asks for a quick interview, to which I agree. At some point during our conversation, I realize I don't have the usual impulse to promote myself, to push the buck so the world will notice what I am up to. I simply listen to his questions and speak about how grateful I am to be here and to see Stacey playing well again. The look on the journalist's face suggests he is wondering if

I am okay. Although he does not say anything, I reply to his unasked question.

"Yes, I am doing amazingly well. I would explain, but I don't think you would understand, as I am not too clear on it myself at this point."

"So we will talk about it later?" he asks.

"Yes, of course," I reply smiling and moving on.

Stacey and I begin to practice, and I sense a real joy and stillness on the court that I have never felt before. When we sit down for a break, I tell Stacey that tennis is so much more than meets the eye. Tennis comes from the heart, I explain, and unless she is fully connected to her heart she will find it very hard to reach the level she aspires to. From her reaction, I can see this is a new concept for her, and it is touching something inside her.

I continue sharing my thoughts.... There is so much more to the game than just hitting the ball well and running the right patterns. That is what people see from the stands, but there is something deeper going on. To reach your flow, you must tap into the place that connects you to what the eye cannot see or the mind understand. It is a place where fear disappears and time stands still. Risk loses its sting and becomes the obvious thing to do. Results and targets lose their importance, as here in this place it's all about being real and being who you are. No more masks or pretenses. No more need to be approved by others.

As I sit here saying all of this, I wonder within me, *Why haven't I shared these things with her before?* I knew about all this stuff before; the difference is that I knew *about* it then, but I didn't *know it personally* as I do now.

At the end of my inspirational speech, I can see in Stacey's eyes the desire to experience this.

"I want this, Pablo. How do I get there?" she asks.

"It's a journey, Stacey," I reply, "and today I believe we have both begun down this road." I explain briefly what I have been experiencing myself. I share with her that the key to finding this flow is "holding on loosely." It's about finding a place of balance between completely surrendering, or giving up, and the need to control everything around us and within us. It's about becoming real, inviting mystery into our lives and enjoying it, and understanding that the Big Guy does not need any help from us.

"Big Guy?" she interrupts.

"Yes the Big Guy, Stace," I reply,

"You mean God?"

"Yes, I do."

"But I don't believe in God, Pablo. You know that."

"Yes, I know that, but He loves us so much that the reality of this place I am speaking about is available and open to anyone who is willing to make the journey. God made us in His image, and because of that we are capable of so much more than the world tells us we are." I explain. "You can take the journey with or without Him.

"God gives us many gifts when He creates us, including the gift of choice," I say. "And God never takes away the gifts He gives us. In other words, He never changes His mind, even if we choose not to acknowledge Him or thank Him for the gifts."

The silence says it all. Stacey has no come back. She realizes something is happening in me, and she definitely wants a piece of the action. We look at each other for a moment, walk to opposite sides of the court and begin to practice.

As I am hitting balls, I begin to wonder if in my excitement I have taken this too far with Stacey. Yet I remind myself that it is okay. For the first time in my life, and certainly in my relationship with God, I feel free to make mistakes.

Resting in the players' lounge for some afternoon reading, I feel the presence of God around me. I have not done anything to deserve it, I have not even invited Him to come join me, but He is here. The lounge is empty, so I close my eyes and pretend to go to sleep. *Oh, this is wonderful,* I think to myself. *Where has this water been all these years?*

"Pablo, I have always been here. The problem is that you have been too busy looking for your own water instead of drinking from what I freely give you," I hear the voice in my heart say. I turn over on the couch; tears flow down my cheeks.

Out of the blue Stacey comes in, and she wants to resume our conversation from this morning. I quickly wipe my tears away and turn around.

"You are crying again?" she asks.

"What do you mean again?" I reply.

"Well, you were crying before breakfast this morning. Weren't you?"

"How did you know?"

"Duh, it was pretty obvious!" she exclaims.

"Well, why didn't you say something then?" I ask.

She shrugs her shoulders and ignores the question. "I want to know what I have to do to start this journey you are talking about," she says with great interest.

"You don't have to do anything except open yourself up and accept the invitation," I reply.

"So, what do I..."

"Stacey, tonight when you are in your room, sit down and stop moving. Stop thinking, and try to let down the barriers of protection around you. Open up and listen to your heart."

"That's it?" she asks.

I laugh. "Yes, that's it."

"And then what?"

"The next step will come when you are ready to take it."

Back at the hotel for the night, Stacey and I talk briefly about tomorrow's match and agree to meet in the lobby at 10 a.m. As we say good-night, she smiles and reminds me she is going to seek the twilight zone when she is back in her room. We laugh together, and as she walks away I whisper a prayer for her.

In my room, I sit down on the big, nice couch. I have been thinking about the Mount of Transfiguration all day, so I open my Bible and start reading about it.

I notice something in these Scriptures that I have never seen before. When I've read this story in the past, I've perceived Jesus meeting Moses and Elijah for a picnic or quiet word. But this time I realize that what is happening here is for the sake of Peter, James and John, whom Jesus has taken with Him.

These three guys are being shown a snapshot, a preview, of what is always going on inside of Jesus. They are witnessing the Life that is taking place inside Jesus every day. Yes, He is there with them physically, but there is another Life inside Him. This incident shows that Jesus is in touch with a place beyond this physical world. This is seen as Moses and Elijah show up. Peter suggests they build three altars to commemorate the occasion, but Jesus dismisses him.

Could this have been nothing more than a normal occurrence to show them something they could not see or understand? And why didn't the other disciples come along? Why only these three? I realize there are other religious reasons why this happened, yet my heart goes on wondering as I close the Bible and get in bed.

I close my eyes, reminding God that all I want is for Him to continue holding my hand and to know He is there. Nothing else. Soon I am asleep.

When I wake up the next morning, I notice the absence of my usual urge to pray and read four chapters of the Bible in order to feel good and somehow engineer the presence of God. I simply lie there in the bed and relish the feeling of being loved, being in a place where all my efforts cease. I stay here for a while enjoying and talking with God. When I finally turn to look at the clock, I realize it's time to get ready for the day's events.

The elevator stops on the fourth floor and several people walk in, greeting me as I acknowledge them. Next it stops on the third floor and Stacey joins us. She sees me back in the corner and smiles.

Reaching the lobby, we all get out. Stacey and I exchange a good-morning, and I ask her how she feels.

"I'm fine, and I am really looking forward to the game to-day," she says, making no mention how last night went for her. Still I can see something has happened, but I choose not to push the issue and simply let her tell me about it when she is ready.

What did I just think? Did I just decide to wait and let her tell me something? Wow, this is definitely new for me. Where are these massive changes coming from? I ask myself.

Not long ago I invaded peoples' lives in the name of concern and wanting to help, even without being invited. I would try fixing people and their situations, trying to manipulate them to become what I thought they needed to be. Without realizing it, I tried to change them so they would succeed and I would look good, thinking that doing so would earn me the love and approval of the world and God Himself.

As we enter the courtesy car for transport to the tournament, Jesus' words, *I do what I see my Father doing,* flash through my mind. *Oh my gosh,* I whisper to myself in near ecstasy, making a connection with Jesus' words and my thoughts. *How did Jesus see? Clearly with His mind, clearly inside of Himself. Could He be describing the Zone? Could He be sharing with us what it is like to be in a place of flowing as one with the Father? A place of being so intimately knitted together with Him that He actually thinks through us. Yes, that's right,* I reaffirm to myself. *That's what it means to have the mind of Christ in us. After all, the Father was in Christ reconciling the world to Himself. By instructing us to take up our cross and follow Him, He meant for us to let go of what we see and what we think we should do or not do. This is an invitation to surrender in order to come to a higher place.* The Scripture in Isaiah 55 about His ways and thoughts being higher than ours suddenly begins to make sense to me.

As we reach the tournament site, I don't want to get out of the car. I just want to keep myself there in that moment. But the driver has other people to pick up, so I oblige him and get out of the car.

Stacey and I warm up, then we sit down to discuss the match, something we always do before her games. I want this conversation to be different; I want to offer more than tactics. As I am wondering how am I going to accomplish this Stacey speaks first.

With an underlying excitement in her voice, she says, "Pablo, I did what you spoke about last night."

"Oh yes, and...?" I reply.

"Well, it was certainly different than anything I have done before. At first I could not quiet myself or stay still long enough. I decided to put some music on my iPod and try again," she said. I am listening like I have never listened before. "Out of the blue, I began to cry, Pablo."

"Really?" I ask with amazement.

"Yes, I began to realize how lonely I am and how much effort I waste trying to please others, including you."

With this I feel like a ton of rocks has just descended on me.

"But the amazing thing is, Pablo, since a few weeks ago I no longer feel that coming from you."

The ton of rocks departs as she continues.

"I began to feel like giving up, to stop trying to force things so much and to simply invite things to come along as they will. To deal with things as they present themselves instead of trying to control everything. I mean, who am I kidding, thinking I can control everything, right?"

"Right," I respond, thanking her for sharing this with me and telling her I am amazed by her experience.

"Really?" she asks, with a puzzled look.

"Yes, really. You know, Stacey, with this idea of 'giving up,' you're really close to a huge breakthrough. But can I suggest something?"

"Sure," she says.

"There is a *world* of difference between 'giving up' and 'holding on loosely.' Remember that term I used when we talked yesterday by the court?"

"Yes" she replies.

"Control, as you're finding, works for awhile, but it has real limits in both tennis and life. 'Giving up' is the opposite, and giving up doesn't work in tennis or in life either. There is something really important in the tension between control and giving up—and that place between the two is called 'the Zone.' When you move from control to giving up, you pass through the Zone, and many people first experience the Zone when they give up and accidentally pass through it. But the truth is, there is a way to enter the Zone intentionally. If I coach you well, you'll know how to find the Zone and play from there."

I encourage her to play this match by holding on loosely instead of trying to control everything. She agrees to give it a try, we quickly go over a few tactics, then she heads off to the locker room.

I sit there amazed not only by what Stacey has just told me but more so by the fact that all this has happened without any real effort on my part. I've simply been open, shared what has been going on in my life and said a short prayer as she and I said good-night the night before. I think back on all those years when I tried to fabricate something like this with very little success. And now all I could hope for and more is happening, not only in my life but also in the lives of those God has brought next to me.

Stacey comes out and plays one of the most amazing matches I have ever seen her play. The level of tennis is scintillating, but even more amazing is the aggressiveness she displays and her self-control in the difficult moments when she would normally panic.

Her performance continues to improve with every match she plays, and soon we find ourselves in the final. With every match she plays, I am more convinced she is understanding more about the Zone. She confesses having a brief moment in one of the matches that felt like an out-of-body experience.

"It was amazing, like I stopped trying and everything was just happening on it's own," she says. "I didn't really need to do anything other than be there.

"The bummer is that it only lasted for a minute."

"That's not unusual at first," I remind her, explaining that now my job is to help her get there intentionally and stay there longer. "I am so excited. What you've done is wonderful, and with each passing day you can become more comfortable being in that place."

Learning to hold on loosely is a journey, a wonderful one, where with time you become aware of the fruits produced in you. It is the place where miracles happen, and when they do, the only part you play is just choosing to be in the Zone instead of being in control or giving up. The miracles become part of your daily life as you begin to notice many things that happen in and around you. You begin to live in the unforced rhythms of grace where lasting change is so obvious that we can even notice it ourselves.

CHAPTER 4

LEARNING TO HOLD ON LOOSELY

Be still and know that I am God.

—Psalm 46:10 (NIV)

In the Hebrew Scriptures, this Psalm is verse 11.

וּפְרָה וְעָדוּ כִּי-אָנֹכִי אֱלֹהִים אָרוּם בַּגּוֹיִם אָרוּם בָּאָרֶץ:

(אי קוסף, ום סיליהת)

וּפְרָה = *"HARPU"* meaning: Hold On Loosely

(Psalm 46:10 in the English translations is Psalm 46:11)

"It was a close one, Pablo. Well done," says a stranger walking by. Stacey had just lost the final in a very close match. It's disappointing as she was leading in both sets. Yet the loss reaffirms in my mind that we are on the right path, but the journey has just begun.

"Well done, Stace. Tough one today," I tell her as we meet in the gym to cool down. The gym is usually very empty on finals day, as only the finalists are still in town. All the other players have departed to the next event on the calendar.

"Urgh! You know I had her, and I should have won the match," Stacey replies, her face showing the obvious disappointment of losing a close match. At times like these, what a coach says to a player can make or break her for the next six months, so I tread carefully as I consider my next words.

"What do you mean by 'I had her?'" I ask, even though I know what she means. I am looking to discover what is going on inside her mind.

"Well, every time I was in the place where I knew I would win the set if I just won the next point, I couldn't keep my mind from rushing ahead of me," she explains. "When I lost that point, then I tried to repair the situation with determination to win the next one at all costs. Fear crept in as I focused on winning the point, and instead of hitting the ball I started trying to push it to be sure it would go in."

Listening to her words, I am hearing what I already suspected was the case from having watched her play. I can tell she is still some distance from understanding what it means to "hold on loosely." She has an innate fear that paralyzes her when she feels she is losing control. Her mind goes into problem-solving mode, and, though the intention is good, the outcome is being controlled by the very thing that she is trying to control.

"Stacey, you have done amazingly well," I say. "You've made much progress, and the most exciting thing is that you are on your way to the place where you will stop trying to control tennis with your mind and start to play it from your heart."

"Pablo, does this state of being really exist?" she asks. "I know you've said I've been playing tennis from a place like this, but what makes you so sure that I wasn't just lucky in those four matches before the final?"

"This state I am helping you to reach is something I am experiencing in my own life, so I know it is there," I assure her.

"You also see it in the movies like *The Last Samurai*. Do you remember the scene in *The Last Samurai* where one of the samurai masters takes Tom Cruise and shows him where the skill comes from?"

"I haven't seen that movie," she replies.

"Well, when Tom Cruise is trying to fight another samurai apprentice, he keeps getting beat by the guy. At a distance, the samurai masters see him struggling. This goes on for days until one of them has had enough and approaches Tom Cruise. He asks him to close his eyes and still try and block the blows this guy throws at him with this wooden sword they use to train," I explain.

"At first he is unable to block the blows and opens his eyes and complains describing the task as nearly impossible. The master shows him that this kind of fighting comes from within him as he points to the place where his heart is. He is asking him to see from inside and feel what is happening," I continue explaining.

"What do you mean? How can that be possible?" Stacey asks, surprised.

"That's what happens when you hold on loosely, as the master tells his student that this kind of skill comes from inside— pointing to the student's chest, not his head." I can see Stacey is processing all of this, so I pause, as I don't want to overload her with information and thus kill the moment.

"I guess I need to watch this movie," she says.

"I think it would be great for you to," I reply. "I have it on my computer; I can lend you my laptop or copy it to yours so you can watch it in the next few days."

Stacey hits the showers, and I head to the restaurant. I have been sitting in the sun for more than two-and-a-half hours watching the match, and I am very tired and starving. I need to get something to eat.

As I wait in line, many people, mostly VIPs, approach me about the match; some even give me "coaching tips" on Stacey's game. Most of their words are going right over my head, although I try to look like I'm listening. It's amazing how easy people find it to judge a situation even though they know little about it. I mean, most of the commentators have only watched this match. They don't know what happened this morning at breakfast; they don't know the emotional and mental factors affecting Stacey at any given time. But here they are telling me how to do my job.

They may know *what* she is doing, but they don't have a clue about *why* she is doing it, so their advice is of little value. Yet I still listen.

Finally making it through the line, I get a sandwich and show the lady at the register my pass. She smiles and waves me by, as she knows who I am after seeing my face for an entire week.

I want to sit away from the crowd where I can be on my own for a bit. Looking around the restaurant, I can see that is not going to be easy, as the place is full of people from the VIP section. I go into the players' lounge, a place where only players, coaches and their guests are admitted. This place would normally be packed, but here on the final day of the event everyone has moved on. I am alone, apart from a few of the tournament staff.

I choose the big couch I have wanted to sit in all week. It has been constantly occupied, so finally I get to feel it under me. As I fall back into it, I pause for a moment and reflect on all that has happened this week. *God, how can I help Stacey understand in practical ways what I am trying to show her—which is the same thing You are showing me?* I pause for a moment to see if I hear or think anything, but my mind is blank. To be honest, I am not surprised as the sandwich is calling my name. I pick it up and open wide. *Finally some food,* I think. As I am about to put my mouth around it, I hear someone scream out my name.

"Pablo! How are you, my boy?" I look up and see a great friend of mine with whom I lost touch many years earlier. I am pleased to see him despite the bad timing, right as I am about to dig my teeth into that juicy sandwich. I can't help but notice that Terry is looking like a million dollars after all these years. Naturally I want to know what has happened, as before we lost touch he was having some devastating problems in his life.

We embrace for what seems an eternity. "It is so good to see you, Pablo," he exclaims.

"It's great to see you too, Terry, and my gosh, you look great, mate," I reply. "Here have a seat. I am about to eat, so would you mind if I stuff myself while we talk?"

"No, of course not, mate. It's the least I can do," he says laughing. "It was great seeing you out there on court. I am so proud of you and how well you are doing for yourself and the player you are coaching."

"Thanks, man. I really appreciate you noticing. We are at a crucial time in her development. She is beginning to learn something that I have learned from my personal experience. If she grasps this, it can take her to the very top," I reply.

"That sounds powerful, Pablo. What is it, if you don't mind my asking?" Terry responds.

"I have been trying to explain to her that, between being in complete control and giving up, there is a state of 'holding on loosely.' In tennis and sports, we call this place the Zone," I explain. This past week, Stacey has been going through this place on her way from total control to giving up, but because of her attempts to control things she is struggling to find that in-between."

Terry nods his head as if he knows exactly what I am talking about. I can tell he is pondering my words, and what I am describing is really resonating with him.

You see Terry went through some very challenging and difficult times in his life. He grew up in a home with a father he describes as a heavenly policeman. No matter what Terry did, it was never good enough or quick enough; there was always something wrong with it according to his father. He never got the smiles and acceptance he wanted from his dad, so he thought the answer was to try harder.

Eventually he became a control freak, as he figured he had to control things or else they were not going to be done well enough. His control became an obsession, and the obsession drove Terry into the ground. He discovered that there was very little in life he could actually control. The more he tried to control, the more he felt out of control. In his endless frustration, he turned to things that could have killed him. But when he met someone who helped him see the root of his need to control, he began to recover his life.

"You know, Pablo, I can really relate to what you are saying as I needed to be delivered from the same struggle Stacey is having," Terry says. "I realized that trying to arm wrestle my own desires simply focused my attention on what I was trying *not* to focus on. It just didn't work. My best efforts to control my life left me out of control. Trying to analyze the situation was no help either; it simply took me out of the moment. Ever notice that you can't think about being a good kisser and, at the same time, kiss someone very well? Either you think about it or you do it, but not both.

"So as Stacey has you, I have a friend who helped me relinquish my attempts to control things."

With that Terry began describing what he had learned from his friend. "He taught me something that helps me to this day —he said control is the willingness to give away everything of value to accomplish a single outcome. He showed me that by my attempts to get specific results by controlling things, I was losing everything that really mattered. I disagreed with him at first, but eventually I saw the truth. In my addictions, I was trying to control parts of life that weren't working, and I was willing to lose everything to hold on to the addictions. The very things I was using in my attempt to control were the things that were taking me out."

Terry continued his explanation, saying that the opposite of control is resignation. "Control isn't working, so I'm gonna take my marbles and go home," he said. "That is resignation, crawling up in the fetal position in a proverbial corner. It happens in someone's soul."

Resignation is not always obvious, Terry pointed out. Some folks who have given in to resignation are the ones living under a bridge, but there are others who have given up in some way at the top of corporations. They show up for life, but something inside them is gone. Resignation is like a form of death.

"Here's the key in what my friend told me," Terry said. "Surrender is the midpoint between control and resignation. Surrender is the tension that admits the desire to control and the desire to resign. Surrender stays in the middle of these two, and it agrees to take the next right step without demanding to know the outcome."

Terry explained that surrender is doing what you know to be right even when you don't know if it will be successful. Surrender is not giving up; surrender is staying fully in the moment, because the result is not the only point. Surrender refuses to sell anything in the moment simply to manipulate a result.

"As I watched Stacey today, I noticed that her tennis technique was good. But she *so* wanted to defeat the opponent that she let her mind slip out of the moment," Terry said. "Her focus became winning and not executing each stroke of the game in the moment. She sold the moment to win the game, and, ironically, it was in trying to win that she lost."

Surrender is the act of being so completely in the moment that the outcome will have to take care of itself.

Terry carried on for the next 30 minutes, but the rest of our meeting, and the day, was a blur to me. We said farewell and promised to stay in touch. As I walked away, I knew I had been given new language for ideas that were as familiar to me as my own two hands.

CHAPTER 5

MAKING IT REAL

If you are a preacher of mercy, do not preach an imaginary but the true mercy. If the mercy is true, you must therefore bear the true, not an imaginary sin. God does not save those who are only imaginary sinners. Be a sinner, and let your sins be strong, but let your trust in Christ be stronger, and rejoice in Christ who is the victor over sin, death, and the world. We will commit sins while we are here, for this life is not a place where justice resides. We, however, says Peter (2 Peter 3:13) are looking forward to a new heaven and a new earth where justice will reign. It suffices that through God's glory we have recognized the Lamb who takes away the sin of the world. No sin can separate us from Him, even if we were to kill or commit adultery thousands of times each day. Do you think such an exalted Lamb paid merely a small price with a meager sacrifice for our sins?

—Martin Luther, 1521

I thank the hotel concierge as he puts my last bag inside the tournament car taking us to the airport.

Stacey and I are going home to rest. We will meet again in two weeks for a training block, as her next tournaments will be played on a different surface than the one she has just been playing on.

As I settle into the back seat of the car, I rehearse the events of the week. Though Stacey made the finals, the high-light of the week was seeing Terry.

The further I walk down this road, the more convinced I am that God is with me for the long haul and not just the first few meters. I am amazed at how He is endorsing every step of the way by clearly answering the questions that come up. What a journey! How different this is from the days when I tried so hard to please Him and earn His love.

Before we part ways, Stacey promises to watch *The Last Samurai* during her break. I know our conversation from the previous day has clearly awakened something in her, and I re-alize that my next task is to help her grasp this state of being and understand how to live in it consistently.

I think of all the things I have learned over the years, all the failures and the triumphs. I try thinking of a way to integrate both my experiences and my new revelation that the only way to experience the transforming Life Jesus spoke about is by learning to hold on loosely.

The courtesy car is gliding down the highway, as it is very early in the morning and there is no traffic. We're riding in a a very nice luxury car. The car is so quiet, I can almost hear my thoughts aloud. I stare out the window; the trees on the side of the road appear to be knitted together into a hedge. The sun is rising on the horizon, and the dew is slowly lifting from the fields along the highway. It's another beautiful morning. Enjoying the views and the ride, I can't help but whisper a prayer to God for help in sharing this revelation with Stacey.

When the car reaches the airport, I thank the driver for the ride and head for the counter to check in. "Good morning, Mr. Giacopelli," greets the lady behind the counter.

"Good morning," I reply with a smile.

"I have some good news for you today. I am going to upgrade you to business class as the flight is full," she says.

"That's great news," I reply, thinking of the 10-hour flight in front of me. I check in my bags and head for the lounge to get something to eat, as I have not had breakfast.

Boy, am I hungry, I think as I approach the food stand on the corner. When the smell of fresh croissants and coffee hits me, I forget completely about my diet and place three fresh chocolate croissants on a plate. My mouth watering like the mouth of a dog that has not eaten for days, I can't wait to get to my seat, so I take a bite from one of the croissants as I pour my coffee.

Returning to my chair to finish eating, I sit back and resume my recollection of all that I have learned in life over the years. I realize that the tremendous amount of time I've spent focusing on my behavior is a symptom of the disease inside me. And continuing to try to fix the symptoms will mean taking on a never-ending job while the disease continues to get worse.

It is so clear from my meeting with Terry that his addictions and obsession to control were symptoms of his disease and not the disease itself.

I finish my last croissant as my flight is called. I am on my way to South Africa to see my children. Little do I know that on this trip I will learn one of the biggest lessons in my life.

I wake up on the plane and realize I have been asleep for almost nine hours. These business class seats are amazing, especially when it comes to long journeys like this one. Though I could sleep another three hours, I get up to stretch. Walking around the plane, I can't help but see the suffering on the faces of the passengers cramped in their economy seats. I have been there, so I know exactly what it feels like.

At the back of the plane, I stretch my legs and peep out of the window to see the most amazing sunrise. *I am so blessed, I think within myself. Not only to have been in business class for this flight, but I am blessed because I am slowly and finally discovering what it really means to live the way we were always meant to. I am learning what has affected me so that I've settled for living in a smaller and meaningless dimension. I am finally relaxing in the presence of the One who is responsible for the beautiful sunrise I just saw and so much more.*

My thoughts turn to my kids, whom I have not seen for several months. It will be a very emotional experience to feel them in my arms again. I think of the undercover cop from heaven they have experienced in me all these years, as I was more preoccupied with their behavior than their heart. This was a by-product of my own off-target approach to having a relationship with God. Thankfully this is all changing as God is revealing His true love and acceptance of me.

Father, please help me to show them Your love and affection for them. Let them see the very Life You are blessing me with, I pray as the cabin supervisor announces that breakfast will be served shortly.

"How long are you planning to stay, sir?" asks the immigration officer.

"Not long enough," I reply with a smile.

"What do you mean sir?" the officer asks with a beautiful African accent and a raised eyebrow.

You see, my family went through a horrible separation as my 17-year relationship with my first wife came sadly to an end. The kids were the victims, of course, as they always are in a divorce. For my kids, it meant their moving to a new country to start a new life without their dad being there with them each day.

Traveling for my job means I am only able to visit every three to four months, and this is not enough for any of us. Still it is what it is, so I am determined to make this time with them different because of all God has been showing me.

I enter the highway to find seven solid lanes of traffic on the four-lane roadway. *Welcome to Africa, the salt of the earth*, I think. I have been on the plane 10 hours, but having been in business class I am feeling fresh and relaxed. Jet lag has not hit me yet, so I choose to enjoy the traffic, if that's possible, and work my way through it to the house where I will be staying.

As I open the door of the car, here comes my son Jake to greet me. This first embrace is always great but painful. "Hey, dad," he says, jumping on me and hugging me so hard that it takes my breath away. As we hold onto one another for a few moments, I whisper, *Thank You, Jesus*. We walk into the house, and I embrace my two daughters, kissing them and smiling as we tell each other how much we have missed being together.

Usually at this stage I would begin to interrogate each of them, especially the older two, about their daily lives and how things are going. I always did this in the name of responsibility. But now I can see I was merely concerned with results and outward behavior so I could feel good and convince myself the kids were okay and the divorce had not affected them the way a divorce normally does. It was a way for me to cover up the guilt my absence brought about, trying to keep God from noticing what was really happening—though in reality He sees and knows everything.

My heart is intent on seeing my children and just being with them. Their bantering and the odd swear word, which in the past has caught my attention, goes right over my head this time. All I want to do is be with them, enjoy them and show real interest in who they are and not how they behave.

I feel so relaxed and I can see they do too. My older daughter, Vanessa, asks me, "Are you okay, Dad?"

"Yes, why Nen (my nickname for her)?" I reply.

They all look at each other and start laughing uncontrollably. "Well, the interviews and questioning haven't started yet, and usually by now you would have told us off a few times for swearing and teasing you about what we've been up to," she says.

My world suddenly stops. Though I reassure them I am more than fine, inside I feel part of me falling away. The old heavenly policeman is leaving, and the loving dad is surfacing.

It strikes me that playing cop was a symptom of my disease and not the disease itself. Holding on loosely means that the things we engineer by our own efforts and good intentions begin to leave our lives so our real selves can begin to surface.

My eyes fill with tears as I think of all the years I have hounded my kids and beat them over the head with a stick in the name of God. I call them all to come, and we embrace again. But this time it is healing.

"I love you guys so much, and I want to say I'm sorry for all these years I have punished you and have never been pleased with you or your behavior," I say. "I want you to know that I love you just as you are. I am not concerned anymore with what you do or don't do, but instead, I want you to know I am interested in who you really are." The room falls silent.

"Dad, really, are you okay? You sure you didn't hit your head on the plane?" asks my son Jake.

"Jake, I want you guys to know that God is not the performance-orientated taskmaster I have shown Him to be," I explain, though I suspect this statement will take some time before it becomes reality to them. Still we have made a start as they obviously already see a big difference in me.

This visit is turning out to be the one I'd hoped for. I feel my love for my children grow. Many situations arise where my commitment to their hearts instead of their behavior is challenged, but I manage to stay the course. I think back on all the past years and what I must have been like to be around.

The sixth day of my visit, I awake very early. I look at the clock; it is only 5 a.m., yet the sun is bright and a cool breeze from the night's gentle rain is coming into the room. From where I am lying on my bed, I can see the golf course. I lie there telling God how grateful I am for all I have and for being able to come into this new dimension of my life and relationship with Him. And I hear Him whisper to me, "This is why I go after your heart, Pablo, and not your behavior."

What do you mean, Lord? I ask.

"You used to think that the better you behaved, the more I loved you, but you see it is the other way around: the more you know I love you, the more you change," He replies.

I get it. The loving comes before the behaving, I think to myself.

"That's right, Pablo," He says.

All this time I have believed that behavior comes before the loving, and it is actually the other way around. Why do we struggle so much to get this basic thing right then? I ask.

"By focusing on behavior, you think you can keep control of the situation. Letting Me love you means that you surrender yourself; what happens depends on Me, not you."

As a parent I understand why most parents want their children to behave in the right way. The problem is that they focus their efforts on affecting and changing their children's behavior instead of their hearts, I respond in my thoughts.

"You see, Pablo, the heart has to come first if behavior is going to change. There is no way that the heart will ever follow behavior."

His words help me realize more than ever that attempting to control behavior is a symptom of disease found in our hearts. Suddenly I understand that everyone wants to be accepted and loved; life teaches us that we need to earn acceptance and love by what we do—be it a job, a career or simply good behavior. But God loves us not because of what we do, the great job we have or how successful we are. He simply loves us. And the best way for us to experience His love is to stop pretending and start being our true selves. As we do so, the "right" behavior will follow as His love changes our hearts. The changes that take place in our hearts will stand the test of time, as they will be changes brought by the hand of God and not through our own efforts.

"Dad, come on. We have to go. Get up," my daughter shouts from her room.

I realize I have just spent two hours talking with God; it felt like 10 minutes. I get up, get ready and take my son and youngest daughter to school and the older daughter to work.

On the way to my daughter's office, we begin to talk about her job. She shares her frustrations, those things she finds really difficult. I listen and offer my point of view as best as I can. As we arrive at her office she turns to me and says, "Dad, that is the first time you have ever listened to me and not stopped me halfway through a sentence to give me your point of view and tell me what you think I should do."

I sit there feeling helpless as we look at each other for what seems an eternity, our eyes glued to each other. Every part of me does not want this moment to end. I smile and hug her as she gets out of the car.

As I drive away, I think back on what just happened. *Where have I been all these years?* I think to myself. *What have I been thinking about not listening to my kids and just being concerned with what I thought was right?*

As I pause my thoughts for a few minutes, I hear God whisper into my heart: "Religion is a terrible thing, Pablo." Tears fill my eyes as I think of all the time I wasted.

"It is okay, Pablo. I make all things new," I hear God whisper, encouraging me.

Yes Lord, I believe that. By now I know this, as it is exactly what He is doing inside my heart.

As my time in South Africa is coming to an end, I decide to treat my children to dinner at a nice restaurant. While we are there I want to thank them for the way they have behaved with me. You see, in past visits my oldest daughter spent much time in the evenings going out with friends. This time she didn't go out once. My son, who on past visits kept most things to himself, made an incredible turnaround; for the first time, we spoke as a father and son are supposed to. My little one cried for the first time as the time for saying good-bye approached, whereas in the past she simply waved from the couch where she was watching TV; if I wanted a kiss from her back then, I had to go to her.

Personally I don't blame my kids for the way they acted towards me. I, too, would have gone out every night, would not have shared anything, would never have shed a tear when it was time to say good-bye.

This visit has been different, as I had hoped and prayed; that's why my kids' reactions have been different. Their reactions have been real, they have come from the heart. And it is because I have been able for the first time to speak to their hearts, all because God is touching mine.

At a nice Italian restaurant we all enjoy, I ask the waiter for a corner table as I want to have some privacy with my kids. As we work our way to the table, we can smell the delicious fresh pasta and bread being served. I am starving, and this smell does nothing to help. But I must do what I have planned, which is to ask my children to forgive me.

As the waiter takes the last order, I hit my glass with my fork. "Guys, I want to tell you something which is not easy, but I believe you will like it," I say. The table now is completely quiet, and all six eyes are zeroed in on me. *Oh God, please help me do this, Lord,* I whisper to myself.

"First, I want to thank you guys for spending so much time with me. I want you three to know I have enjoyed every minute of it. But what I have enjoyed most has been the way we have been able to spend time together. Vanessa, thank you for staying home and taking the time to be with your dad. Jake, thank you for trusting me with your secrets; and, Mia, thank you for smiling so much at me every time you saw me," I continue.

"You see guys, for years I thought God was someone who was never pleased. I thought He always got very disappointed when I made mistakes. I wanted to please Him so much, and yet I always felt I never did. So I tried harder to be perfect; yet the harder I tried, the angrier I got."

"When I saw you guys make similar mistakes to mine and not be the perfect people I thought we had to be, I got very angry. I know it must have been horrible for you to have a dad like that around you."

"Dad, we love you," my older daughter tells me with tears in her eyes. "You have changed so much that we want to be with you. We feel like you like us now and that you are really proud of us."

With her last few words I begin to fill up with emotions; only the waiter bringing the drinks stops me from bursting out in tears. We enjoy a wonderful dinner together, and as we do, I sense the healing hands of God at work in all of us.

The Bible says that what we cannot see is more real than what we see. How very true it is. The healing begun here tonight is something that can't be seen but only felt; the words and the tears are the evidence. Just as the things that kill our hearts have symptoms, so do the things that heal us and give us life. In this case, the words are symptoms of love; the tears are symptoms of healing and joy.

The next day I pack my bags, as it is time to leave for the next tournament. We say our good-byes, and tears flow along with the "I love you's" like they have never flowed before. As I get into the car, my son shouts from his balcony, "Dad, I am really going to miss you." I have heard this from him before, but this time I can hear the words coming straight from his heart to mine.

"Me too, big boy, me too, and more than you know," I reply.

I enter the highway and can't help but think what a wonderful time I have just had with my kids. What an amazing love and affection I felt for them and how unaffected I was by their behavior. I think of all the amazing moments we spent together and of that strange feeling I had in every one of those moments. I was wholly present; there was no past or future, just the moment.

Wow, I think as I meditate on this truth. *That's it. We can't hold on loosely if we are too busy in the past or the future.*

Does that mean we can only find You in the moment, God? I ask with some hesitation.

"That's all you have, Pablo. The moment you are in. Where else can you love Me or find Me, if not in the moment you have right now?"

But You say You are the Beginning and the End and You hold our tomorrows in Your hands, I reply.

"Yes, I do, but you can't be there. You can only be here at this moment. The future is a present that has not yet happened, and the past is a present that already took place."

With this last remark I am silenced. I realize that I have just stumbled upon a massive pearl of wisdom and truth. Little did I know the size of the impact this truth would have in my life and Stacey's in the coming weeks.

I spend the rest of the journey to the airport thinking about what I have just heard. As I sit down on the airplane, I get an email from Stacey on my Blackberry. She has watched the movie I recommended and can't wait to talk to me about it. Neither can I wait to talk to her about all I have learned these past two weeks.

"Flight attendants, please be seated for takeoff," the captain announces over the intercom.

Here we go again, baby!

CHAPTER 6

BEING PRESENT

*Then Moses said to God, "Suppose I go to the People of Israel
and I tell them, 'The God of your fathers sent me to you'; and
they ask me, 'What is his name?' What do I tell them?"*

*God said to Moses, "**I AM WHO I AM**. Tell the People of
Israel, '**I AM** sent me to you.'"*

—Exodus 3:13–14 (emphasis added)

*"Give your entire attention to what God is doing right now,
and don't get worked up about what may or may not happen
tomorrow. God will help you deal with whatever hard things
come up when the time comes."*

—Matthew 6:34

"Sir, please fasten your seat belt as we are landing soon," the flight attendant says to me as I wake up. I have literally slept the whole flight, 10 hours, in an economy seat as if it was my own bed. Some friends tell me my ability to do this is unreal. Truth be told, it is something I have learned to do, as it is either sleep or stay awake watching everyone else sleep for 10 hours. So the right choice is pretty obvious in my mind. Getting a window seat is the key to success, as that way I'm able to lean on the side of the plane and rest without worrying about waking up face-to-face with the hairy man sitting next to me.

As the plane taxis to the terminal, I think of Stacey and our reunion that will take place at the hotel in a few hours. Since she arrived last night, I expect she will be waiting for me, eager to talk about the movie she watched during the break.

I have learned so much from all that has happened in these last two weeks. I am anxious about communicating these things to her clearly and slowly, without being overtaken by my enthusiasm. *Lord, please help me to know what to say and when to say it,* I whisper to God as I walk down the aisle of the plane and head for the terminal.

It is very early in the morning, and ours is the first international flight to arrive. The terminal is very quiet. As I look around the nearly silent terminal en route to baggage claim, I notice all the advertisements that fill the halls. *Airports are looking more and more like the highways,* I think to myself. One poster in particular catches my attention. It is advertising some sort of consulting company, and in big, bright letters it says "Stay Present." *There it is again,* I think, remembering how Jesus speaks this message in the Bible.

On the way from the airport to the hotel, I get out my Bible to look up these references. Matthew 6 comes to mind. I find it and begin to read it. When I reach verse 30, the words practically jump off the page. Jesus is speaking, and here is how *The Message* paraphrases His words:

> *30-33If God gives such attention to the appearance of wildflowers—most of which are never even seen—don't you think he'll attend to you, take pride in you, do his best for you? What I'm trying to do here is to get you to relax, to not be so preoccupied with getting, so you can respond to God's giving. People who don't know God and the way he works fuss over these things, but you know both God and how he works. Steep your life in God-reality, God-initiative, God-provisions. Don't worry about missing out. You'll find all your everyday human concerns will be met.*
>
> *34 Give your entire attention to what God is doing right now, and don't get worked up about what may or may not happen tomorrow. God will help you deal with whatever hard things come up when the time comes.*
>
> (Matthew 6:30–34)

I understand Jesus is not only telling us not to worry about the future but to also live one day at a time. How often I catch myself worrying about things that might happen, then planning my response as though I can control things, and this is before the situation has ever occurred.

Why do I do this, God? I ask, as I lean my head back on the headrest of the courtesy car taking me to the tournament.

"Reading anything interesting?" the driver asks.

"It depends what you mean by interesting," I reply. Before I have a chance to explain, his radio interrupts.

"Excuse me," he says, as he turns his attention to the call from the tournament base.

I look back at the passage I have just read. The word *getting* keeps jumping out at me. *What is it about getting that has to do with staying present?* I continue to read and see the word *giving,* the complete opposite of getting.

I am confused, God. Please help me see what these two things have to do with being present.

"It has to do with your ego, Pablo," I hear in my heart.

Ego? I ask.

"Yes, your ego."

Suddenly in the back seat of that courtesy car, I have one of those life-changing moments where my understanding breaks through to a new level. "I get it!" I shout with delight, alarming the driver who nearly swerves off the road.

For the first time in my life, I realize that when you are present in the moment there is no place for ego. When you are fully present in that moment with your mind, heart and whole being, you are not aware of the past or the future. Ego lives in the past or the future, striving and toiling to "get" something as though we have control of our lives. Ego is about trying to find and ensure our security, thinking that if we just get this or that, then everything will be fine. In reality, we have very little control of anything in life.

Giving, on the other hand, is living with an attitude of surrender or holding on loosely. We live with the understanding that we do what we can but the result is not up to us. We do what we know to do in the moment without worry about what has been or is to come.

That's why we worry, I think. *That's why Jesus tells us not to worry but to relax and give our entire attention to what God is doing right now.*

I think of all those years I spent worrying about the future, about what I would do, how I would manage if this or that happened. Even when I was supposedly relaxing, I was always attempting to manipulate my circumstances, forcing things, trying to get as much as possible. *I must have missed so much of God's giving.*

"We are here, sir," says the driver.

Thank you very much," I respond as I get out of the car. I grab my bags and enter the lobby to check into what will be my home for the next seven days. No sooner have I walked through the spinning door than I hear, "Pabloooo!"

It's Stacey. I look at her and can see she is happy and relaxed. As we embrace, I tell her how happy I am to see her.

"I have so much to tell you," Stacey says, full of excitement. "I watched *The Last Samurai* and liked it so much because, of course, you know I just adore Tom Cruise. He is so hot, oh my gosh!"

"Stacey, try and breathe," I tell her as she is talking a million miles an hour. The lady at registration calls me up to the desk. "Okay, let me check in and then we can have a chat."

"Okay, cool," Stacey says. "See you in half an hour then?"

"Yep, that works," I reply.

I catch the elevator, and when I reach my room, I am welcomed by a voice saying, "Welcome to your room, Mr. Giacopelli." My imagination runs away with me, thinking I am going to have a personal attendant for the week. But my hopes are dashed as I see my name flash across the television screen as the greeting message repeats. I turn it off and lie down on the bed, which I can safely say is the biggest bed I have ever seen in my life.

I take a quick shower and change clothes. I'll be meeting Stacey in just a few minutes, so I quickly ask God to help me communicate to her all I have learned in these past two weeks.

"Stay present as you talk to her," I hear God whisper into my heart.

Yes, I think, *that's a great idea as I have a habit of thinking of what I am going to say instead of focusing on what I am actually saying at that moment in time.*

"I will have water, please," I tell the waiter as Stacey and I meet in the restaurant. "So Stacey, I can see you have lots to tell me. Please go ahead."

She jumps right into telling me her impressions of *The Last Samurai*, saying that it really spoke to her.

"Okay, that's fine," I say, thinking of what an amazing impact one actor can have on someone. I guess that is why some of them are paid so much money.

"The whole movie was just amazing. I loved the way Tom Cruise's character slowly but surely becomes one of the clan by living with the others and interacting with them. The part that really spoke to me, though, was when he is learning the ways of the samurai. I remembered what you had told me. You know the part where they are all in the field, and the teacher tells him that he has too much in his head and tells him to just let go by closing his eyes?" she explains.

"Yes, I sure do Stace," I reply with great delight, as I can see she has gained new understanding.

"It's amazing, because as he does that and lets go of trying to control his every movement, and especially the samurai itself, he is able to fight this guy who keeps kicking his ass. But the most amazing thing, Pablo, is that he doesn't get it straight away. It takes him time, but the awesome thing is that he gets it, he understands in that moment what you have been trying to tell me. He finds that place of holding on loosely," she says.

"Oh, Stacey, this is fantastic, darling," I tell her with excitement. "I am so proud of you, that you were able to pick up on this the first time you watched the movie."

"I saw the same thing with another movie I watched since this one, but it was *The Last Samurai* that really did it for me," she says.

"And I guess Tom Cruise also had something to do with it?" I ask with a smile.

"Oh yes, definitely," she responds laughing.

"Stacey, I have been doing some learning too, and I want to share with you a couple of things that are very much in line with a scene from *The Last Samurai*," I tell her, silently praying for God's help. "In that scene where Tom Cruise finally gets it, what is the teacher essentially asking him to do?"

"To stop thinking about how he uses the sword and just do it," she replies.

"That's right. So in other words he needs to stop thinking about every movement he is making or that he is going to make after the current one. This basically paralyses him as he is focusing on something that has not happened yet, which is the next move. He is trying to control things. However, the more he tries to control, the worse he gets at it." I explain. "Are you with me so far?"

"Yes, I sure am," Stacey replies.

"Now, do you remember a bit before that when he wants to give up? This happens the harder he tries. Then he realizes he is trying to control things. He moves from one extreme, giving up, to the other, trying to control," I ask her.

"Yes, I remember that," she replies, surprising me as she continues. "And the amazing thing is that as long as he kept trying to approach the samurai thinking it was just like firing a gun or like he fought his wars, the harder it was for him to get it."

"Wow, Stacey, what you have just said is very powerful," I reply. "So, what you are saying is that we have to come to a place where we realize that we have control of very little and understand that when we stop trying to control things we are not giving up. What we are doing is welcoming mystery into our lives."

"Yes, it's like we can't do it if we don't let go of the outcome and just focus on the process," she says.

"So what other way would or could you describe what Tom Cruise is having to do as he lets go and holds on loosely?" I ask.

"Well, if he has to stop thinking about the next step or what has happened before, then he can only be in the moment, be present, not somewhere else," she answers.

"That's right, Stacey. You got it!" I exclaim. "Now, what are the things that dominate a tennis player's mind when she is out there playing if she is not in the moment?" I ask.

"Winning and losing" she responds immediately.

"That's right. And what do you do when things start looking like they are about to escape your control?" I ask.

"Well, I do two things. First, I try to figure out a way I can keep control. I think of a way of playing the point, but as soon as I do, my mind reminds me I lost the point the last time I tried that. Then I think of the score and imagine what it will be like if I lose this next point. As soon as I do this, I begin to get scared as I don't like the fact that so much is hanging on the next point," she says.

"Amazing, isn't it, Stacey, that the whole time you are everywhere else but in the moment? Your mind is in the past, then the future, then fear and worry creep in and start to paralyze you, and nine times out of ten you end up losing the point. Your worst fears come to pass."

"Yes, that's right, Pablo. That's exactly right. It's like I am scared to accept that I have no control of the outcome," she says. As I look at her, I can see that she is having one of those moments like I had in the car on the way to the hotel. "So does that mean I have to invite mystery into my life and just accept whatever mystery brings—in other words, whichever way the result goes?" she asks.

"That's right, Stacey. Well done. You got it all in one," I reply. "This is what it is all about. You focus on what is in front of you, playing the tactic we agreed on with the same intensity and commitment you played all those other points when maybe you were not at risk of losing. Focusing only on that point, one ball at a time, not the result," I tell her. "Just like Tom Cruise. Let it come from the heart, not from the mind; let it flow out of you, and stop getting in the way by trying to manipulate it and control it."

We sit there looking at each other as if we both know we have just had a life-changing conversation. We have both been visited by truth, and I know we will never be the same because of it.

I finish sipping my water, and we return to our rooms to get ready for practice. In two hours, we are playing a practice set with a very good player, which will be a perfect place for Stacey to try her hand at what we have just been talking about.

On the way to the courts, Stacey tells me that her boyfriend's birthday is in a few weeks. She is worried because she hasn't bought him anything yet, and she doesn't know how she is going to get it done in time as she doesn't even know what she is going to buy him.

"Stacey, you know what we just talked about in the restaurant, about staying present?" I ask.

She starts to laugh as she says, "Yes, I know. I am somewhere else again instead of being in the moment."

"That's right. These things we are talking about are a way of life, Stacey. You don't have to be on a tennis court or in a match to practice them and experience the benefits in your life. These things are so powerful that anyone can use them at any time and enjoy the release and freedom they bring," I explain.

As our trip continues, I realize I am the first one who should be taking notes and listening to what I have just told Stacey, especially when I sit down to watch her matches. You see, for a tennis coach, watching a match of the player one works with is like watching someone give birth. You feel completely helpless. You can do very little about the outcome of either event. In the past, my mind has played so many games with me as I watched matches, thinking of ways to force the outcome I wanted, which was obviously a victory for Stacey.

The whole subject of ego once again flashes through my mind. If I am honest, I can see that the only reason, why I try to control the outcome of a match so that my player wins and, as her coach, I will look good. I know this might sound strange, but there are very few coaches (or church leaders, for that matter) who only want others to succeed and prosper without a driving desire to make themselves look good in the process. What appeals to my ego—and has done so for most of my life, both as a player and a coach—is looking good on the outside. It is not just about being a winner or having a winning player; it comes down to making more money so I can buy better things and do things I can't do now. Ego always keeps me somewhere else, thinking about getting rather than the giving that could be done each moment of my life. It always diverts me away from the moment toward other things or events, as that is where ego gets its power to survive.

Being present means that I am still, just as Psalm 46 describes "Be still and know that I am God." In other words, be present and don't worry about the future. Be present, and don't worry about what might or might not happen. Be present, and leave the result and the outcome to God. Be present, and see what God is doing in you, through you and around you. Be present, and see what Jesus meant when He told us in Mattew 6 not to worry.

"Ok, we are here," the driver of our car, announces as we pull up to the entrance of the tournament venue.

CHAPTER 7

FRIENDS FOR THE JOURNEY

... In each of my friends there is something that only some other friend can fully bring out. By myself I am not large enough to call the whole man into being...

—*C.S. Lewis*

"Wow! What a beautiful day," I exclaim as Stacey and I exit the clubhouse on our way to the court to practice. Though it is a cloudless day, it is windy, and Stacey notices.

"I hate the wind," she says, providing the perfect opportunity for me to encourage her to stay in the moment and let go of things she cannot control.

"Amazing, isn't it? Every time we talk about something, an opportunity to put it into practice soon presents itself," she replies with a cheeky smile on her face.

"I know. It's almost as if Someone we can't see is listening and setting up exercises for you to learn in a practical way," I reply with an even cheekier smile on my face. We both laugh, as we know deep inside this is something we are learning together as we go.

"Stacey, finish your warm-up while I run back to the clubhouse. I forgot the balls. I will be right back," I say.

As I climb the stairs, I think about how grateful I am for everything God is doing with my life and through it. It is amazing that the more I choose to hold on loosely and live in the moment, the more positive changes I see taking place in my life and the lives of those around me. The very presence of God shows up to people when I show up and pour out His love and life to them. All because I am getting my ego out of the way, happy to tag along with Him and watch Him do what only He can do, which is to bring abundant Life to everyone He touches.

After a couple hours, Stacey finishes her practice. "Great work," I tell her. "How did that feel?" It's the first practice she's had since our conversation at the hotel, and I'm dying to know what difference it has made for her.

"Well, at the beginning, I was not enjoying it at all as I was just thinking about how much I hated the wind. But after you spoke to me, I began to let go of the thought that the practice would not go well because of the wind. I felt a release inside that helped me to focus on one ball at a time, and suddenly everything started to flow. I quite like the wind now," she replied with a great big smile on her face.

Thanking the practice partner and her team, we head off the court, and Terry meets us at the gate. I see his familiar face out of the corner of my eye. "Terry, what's going on mate? Fancy seeing you here," I exclaim.

"I am here on business for the week, and I heard you were in town," he said. "So I came down to the tournament to see if I could spend some time with you and find out how you are getting along and lend you some support."

"That's great!" I reply. "Terry, please meet Stacey."

"Hello, Stacey. Nice to meet you. How are you?" Terry asks.

"I am doing very well," Stacey replies.

"This is the friend of mine I told you about, the one I saw at the event before we went on our break," I explain to Stacey.

The three of us walk toward the players' lounge and agree to have dinner together. "Stacey, go and get ready, and Terry and I will wait for you here," I say.

"Okay, cool. I will be right back," Stacey replies.

Terry and I grab something to drink and sit down to wait for her. No sooner have we taken our seats than Stacey reappears.

"Okay guys, I am ready; let's go. I am starving," she says. Terry and I laugh as we get up to go and catch the car that will drive us to the restaurant.

I look out the window of the car on our route. I've been to this restaurant before, and I am amazed at how this town has grown. There are new buildings everywhere.

Thank you, Lord, for bringing Terry into our lives, I whisper to God, realizing there was nothing I could have done to make this happen. It is amazing to have Terry with us, sharing his own journey of deliverance, how he learned to live by holding on loosely. I smile again as I think of all those years I tried so hard but failed to make things happen. I remember how I tried so hard yet never got the results I wanted. I blamed myself, believing everything was up to me. Yet now, as I am learning to hold on loosely and to not worry about the results but enjoy the process, I realize how, little by little, everything is falling into place. But most importantly, I realize how different this way of life really is, how different I feel inside and view life and God.

I see obstacles in a different light now. Whereas before I used to see God intentionally making things difficult for me, now I see the situations as opportunities to learn something new about Him and the love He has for me. I see opportunities to strengthen my resolve to hold on loosely and enjoy the ride regardless of what is happening.

"We are here," announces the driver.

"Yep, that's the one," I say as I look up to see the Old Italian restaurant.

"What time should I pick you up for the trip back to the hotel?" asks the driver.

I look back at Terry and Stacey, and we all start laughing as we know we could be there for hours. "Don't worry," I tell him. "We will catch a cab home. Thank you very much for all your help."

As soon as we step in the door, the wonderful smell of homemade Italian food hits us. The place looks exactly the same as the last time I was here. So do the waitresses and the owner, Massimo, who, much to my surprise, remembers me.

"Pablo!" he shouts across the restaurant with a heavy Italian accent.

"Hello, Massimo. I can't believe you remember me. It has been three years since I was last here," I reply as we embrace the good Old Italian way.

"I never forget someone like you, my boy," Massimo replies. "I have waited each year, hoping you would come back, but realized as the days went by that you had not come. But now, here you are!"

"Massimo, this is the player I am working with, Stacey, and my very good friend Terry."

"Ah! If you are Pablo's friends, then you are my friends too!" he replies as we all walk through the restaurant to our table.

By now everyone in the place is staring at us, especially at Stacey, as most of them are tennis fans who spent the day watching players practice.

"Massimo, can we have the private room as we need to talk?" I ask.

"But, of course, my friend. For you, I do anything," he replies, winking at me.

"Thank you very much. I really appreciate it!"

We sit down, and Massimo gives us the menus and tells us about the specials. He highly recommends we try the ravioli, explaining they have a new chef who makes some really amazing ravioli.

"Are you having wine with that?" he asks.

Stacey and I both look at Terry simultaneously, and we all start to laugh. "No, we will have water, Massimo. Thanks!" I reply.

"So, how has it been going guys?" Terry asks.

"It's going very well. Since we last spoke, we have come a long way in understanding how to hold on loosely," I reply, looking at Stacey who remains quiet.

"Ah yes, holding on loosely. I love that saying, Pablo," Terry responds as our waitress brings the drinks. "You know, not long ago I took some dancing lessons. I wanted to learn how to dance with someone else, so I signed up for this class. I will never forget the first lesson. Here I was with this lady in front of me, someone I had never seen before in my life. Every time I had watched couples dance it looked to me like the man had firm control of his partner. So I naturally assumed I would need to control this lady, almost forcefully, when I danced with her. I tried but failed miserably," Terry said with a smile on his face.

"The teacher came over, looked me in the eyes, and in-structed me not to hold my partner so tight. She explained that leading her did not mean ordering her around. In fact, she said that by holding her more loosely I would make it easier for her to adapt to my lead and for us to flow from step to step. I thought okay, no problem; so off I went. Of course I soon real-ized that attempting to control was not just part of my dancing but very much part of my nature, so it took time and many les-sons until I was able to relax enough that I could truly dance.

"You see, Stacey, the way I danced was the same way I lived. The way you play tennis is also the same way you live. I am sure that you, like me, have good and genuine reasons why you live as you do. However, life was not meant to be lived these ways we have been living. By trying to do it our way, we end up broken, frustrated and often controlled by the very things we are trying to control in the first place. This is how many people end up addicted to alcohol or drugs," Terry said.

Our conversation is temporarily interrupted by the wait-ress bringing our meals. "Do you mind if I tell you a bit of my story while we eat?" Terry asks Stacey.

"Not at all. Please do, Terry," she replies.

"I was born to a father whom I found hard to please. He was like a heavenly policeman," Terry begins. "It didn't matter what I did or how I did it, I never seemed to get the nod of ap-proval. As the years went by, I grew more and more desper-ate to get my dad to smile and say well-done. Yet the harder I tried, the further away I seemed to move from this goal. In time, my dad's approval became the mission of my life. Even after I left home, I was still trying to subconsciously please my father, and my need for approval transferred to other people as well.

"As you know, Stacey, approval is hard to get, and even when you manage to get it, it is usually conditional and superficial. As the circumstances change, so does others' approval.

"Life went by, and I found myself running out of energy, like a hamster running inside a wheel. Yes, there was a lot of action in my life, but there was no motion whatsoever.

"In my inability to control situations, I began looking for things to help me cope, somehow forget, or even ignore the reality of my failures. I thought I was creating a situation that would make me feel like I had succeeded in gaining control of something," Terry continued.

"I began to mix with the wrong crowds, and soon after that I began to drink. The drinking was social at first, but soon it became my crutch. During the early years, I believed it gave me the escape route I needed to feel in control, as I was able to numb the pain and avoid the wound inside me. Somehow I felt like I had control of the situation, but in reality, the more I drank, the more I became controlled by it."

As we finish our main courses, the waitress comes in and asks if we would like dessert or coffee.

"Oh yes, I strongly recommend, this guys," I say, looking at both Stacey and Terry. "You have to try the tiramisu!"

"Okay. Let's have three, then," Terry says to the waitress.

"I will also have a tea, please," I ask, as Terry resumes his story.

"My life deteriorated very fast from this point. I lost my job and all contact with my family, as I became a shame to them and their religious pride. I remember going to the ATM to get cash only to find that my account had been cancelled. My situation became desperate and low.

Then one day I met a guy in a club and we started to talk. He listened to my stories and could even relate to them, though deep down he knew what was really happening in my life. After hanging out with this guy for awhile, I began to realize that my drinking was not my problem. Instead, it was only a symptom. My need to control every situation in my life so that I could please others and earn their approval and acceptance was the real problem. Strangers weren't really the ones I wanted to see smile at me, but when they did it somehow comforted the wound caused by my father's withholding. I substituted their smiles for my father's smile that I really longed for.

"The healing began to flow in my life as I started learning to 'hold on loosely' as Pablo says. Soon my friend from the club helped me let go of the need to control. The more I held on loosely, the less attractive the need to control became. In time I realized that my father had only been doing to me what had been done to him. You see, even religion can be a way of trying to control things, including, as crazy as it sounds, trying to control God. I mean, can you imagine that, trying to control God?" Terry asks with a smile.

We all laugh, though sadly I realize this is what I was trying to do not long ago. I feel blessed that I can actually laugh about it now.

"Today, Stacey, I have been given the things I was so desperate to get back then," Terry adds. "My father and I have reconciled our relationship. I have a better job and better material possessions than I ever did before, even though I worked twice as hard back then as I do now.

"What Pablo is sharing with you is very powerful, Stacey. It will transform not only your tennis career but also your whole life. The important thing is to have someone next to you who will go through this process of leaving the pier of control and sailing into the ocean of holding on loosely. It is not an easy sail, hence the need for help to keep you honest and encouraged. There will be many days when you will want to return to what is familiar to you. The problem is that the familiar will be the very things that limit you from becoming all you were meant to be. These things will be responsible for stopping you from fully enjoying and experiencing the dance called 'your life.'"

With this, Terry stops talking and looks at both Stacey and me. We sit there for what seems an eternity. The room has become very warm, as Terry's story has cut right through our hearts without asking permission. It is as if we are in eternity for a moment in time.

The waitress eventually interrupts the moment, asking "Would you like the bill?"

"Yes, I will be taking care of that," Terry says.

We stay a bit longer, chatting about the day ahead, and then head out to catch a taxi back to the hotel.

We embrace Terry to say goodbye. "Thank you, Pablo, for tonight, for listening and for being a real friend," he says looking me in the eyes.

"It is not hard when you hold on loosely, Ter," I reply, laughing as we go our separate ways.

I walk away profoundly impacted by Terry's journey, the powerful deliverance and turnaround in his life. I also realize more than ever how important it is to have someone next to you who is able to walk with you during these times of change. In particular, changes in our hearts, such as learning to hold on loosely, can be very painful and frustrating journeys.

Oh Lord, I have become so fixed and obsessed with the outcome of everything in my life, I pray as I sit on my bed back in the hotel room.

"Even in your relationship with Me," God whispers into my heart.

What do you mean, Lord? I ask.

"Pablo, every time you have approached Me, you have come with a real sense of entitlement in your heart of what you believed I should do or give to you. If I didn't deliver, you felt betrayed and shortchanged. This frustration increased as time went by, especially when you didn't get what you thought you deserved or was naturally due to you," He continued.

"You see, entitlement is rooted in the need to control every-thing in your life. In the religious world, they call it 'name and claim it.' The more you focus on these quick-fix schemes, the more you lose sight of what I really want for you. What I want for you is a relationship not based on performance or behavior but one that is based on My love for you."

By this time I am nearly in tears as I realize how selfish and self-centered I have been with God. Suddenly it becomes clear to me why I have always felt my relationship with Him was somewhat forced and that He was always absent. I mean, come on, who wants to be in a relationship where you are forced to do what the other person wants and you can't be who you really are?

"Pablo, it doesn't end there, son," He whispers.

What do You mean? I ask.

"As well as your need to control what I gave you and what you thought I should do for you, you also tried to control the way I spoke to you, when I spoke to you, what I said to you, how I should behave, and even when I should show up in your life," He said.

As He says this, I see a mental picture of me walking God on a leash. I realize this is how I have been approaching my relationship with God all along, and I finally understand why it never worked and only felt like hard work.

Please show me how to change, I ask. Immediately I see in my mind the leash that was holding Him break. Then He begins to run around me. He comes alive, runs away and calls me to come find Him. As I do and am about to catch Him, He leads me somewhere else. This goes on in my mind for several minutes before He tells me to stop.

"Did you enjoy that?" He asks me.

Yes, I really did. I loved it, I reply.

"Now son, look back," He says.

In my mind, I turn around and look. I see that each place He led me was a place I longed to be, a place where great things happened, a place where I accomplished things far beyond what I could ask for or imagine. *Wow, this is so cool.*

"Yes, and the coolest thing is that you never focused on controlling me or where I took you, but instead you focused on Me and allowed Me to lead you. That's what holding on loosely is about Pablo. It's about relaxing so you can receive what I am always giving you, instead of trying to force Me to provide you with what you think you need or deserve.

Opening my eyes, the first thing I want to know is where in Scripture I can find what God has just told me. So I ask and, once again, Matthew 6 comes to mind. I open the Bible and look back at the passage I was looking at just previously in *The Message*. Verses 32 and 33 jump out at me, and I sense God speaking to me through them again.

What I'm trying to do here is to get you to relax, to not be so preoccupied with getting, so you can respond to God's giving. People who don't know God and the way he works fuss over these things, but you know both God and how he works. Steep your life in God-reality, God-initiative, God-provisions. Don't worry about missing out. You'll find all your everyday human concerns will be met.

Oh, now I get it, Lord! Thank You for all you are doing in my life.

I turn the lights off. As I turn over in the bed and my head hits the pillow, I fall asleep resting securely in the arms of my Father in Heaven, realizing that He is taking me on the greatest journey. Just like the dance instructor led Terry, God is leading me as we dance together to the beat of the life He has planned for me. Finally, I am starting to understand that I can fully trust Him, wherever He might lead me next.

CHAPTER 8

RIPPLE EFFECT

Some things are caught, not taught.

—Anonymous

I wake up early the next morning, as I want to spend some time on my own walking by the ocean. It is going to be an interesting day, and I need some quiet time to prepare for it.

In the past, I would have spent no more than four or five minutes with God in the morning, mainly because the time was dry and lifeless and I could hardly get myself through it. After the obligatory minutes, I would have started my routine preparations for the day, including formulating the answers I would give to the questions I expected to be asked.

Now, don't get me wrong. Being prepared is a good thing; however, if your own preparation is all you rely on, then I believe your answers will more than likely be manipulating those who are asking you the questions. These days, as I am learning to live by holding on loosely, I understand more and more what it means and how it looks when it is happening.

As I walk out of the hotel, the fresh scent of the ocean reminds me of childhood summer days spent at the beach with my mother. My father often traveled with his job, so he usually did not accompany us on the beach trips.

I walk out to the pier in search of the spot I found three years ago. It was the perfect place for watching the sun set.

The ocean is calm this morning. I close my eyes and enjoy the gentle summer breeze. I hear the waves breaking on the shore one after another. As I walk the beach, I stare into the horizon and thank God for this moment. My mind is nowhere else but here. My heart is swelling with gratitude; my mouth, half-open in awe. I sense the overwhelming presence of God, but this is nothing like a religious meeting. God is here in the gentle ocean waves, the cool breeze, the colorful horizon and the sun that is rising for a brand new day.

I spend the next 45 minutes simply walking and enjoying God's presence. These days it is easy to recognize Him, as I am not forcing Him to fit into my agenda or pretending to be someone I am not. Instead I am walking with my Father in heaven, enjoying what He has made. I'm also increasing in the understanding of how much He loves me and wants to spend quality time with me.

As I return to the hotel, I see Stacey sitting alone outside on the balcony. I am not sure if she has seen me. She looks as though she is having one of those moments when truth illuminates the darkness and brings freedom to the heart. So I decide to walk around to the back entrance of the hotel and leave her to it. In the past, I would have butted in, but I am slowly learning that God does not need my help, He can sort things out on His own. In fact, I will later find out how right I am not to interrupt Stacey and this precious moment she is having.

Back at my room, I shower and get ready to meet Stacey for breakfast.

"Good morning, Stacey. How are you today?" I ask as I approach her in the lobby where there are some other people walking around.

"Pablo, do you mind if we have breakfast outside on our own?" she asks.

"I don't see why not, Stace. Are you okay?" I reply.

"I am not sure I know how to answer that right now," she replies with a smile. "I know I am more than okay, but this is all so new. I did something this morning that I never thought I would do."

I immediately assume she is talking about the time she spent outside on the balcony this morning. But I stay silent, choosing to let her tell me what is in her heart. After all, this is her moment, not mine.

We find a table outside near the spot where I saw her sitting alone earlier. After getting our breakfast from the buffet, we sit down and begin to talk. The sun is now shining brightly and the temperature has increased, though it is still very nice to be outside. The breeze I felt during my walk on the beach is still around.

"I don't know where to start, Pablo," Stacey says.

"Well, how about with what is on your heart this very moment, Stace?" I reply.

"Last night after we got back to the hotel, I went to my room and sat there for hours just staring out of the window into the night sky. I thought about everything Terry said at dinner and how it seemed amazingly like he was speaking directly to me. I realized at the restaurant, though I didn't say anything, that I have been performing to earn and keep my father's affection, to see him happy when I do well, just like Terry described in his own life.

"I loved it when Terry explained how his friend told him his own similar story so Terry would feel safe and not ashamed of who he was and the problems he had," she says. "You know, Terry did that for me last night. And the amazing thing is, I don't even know if he was trying to do that. Yet I felt so safe that I was able to reflect on my heart and the wound I have been carrying inside all of my life.

"For the first time, I could see why I have been trying to control everything around me. It was about trying to obtain the outcome I thought I needed in order for my dad to love and accept me. In fact, I realized that fear is underneath my attempts to control; that is why I panic on the court and rush ahead in my mind to find solutions. The fear keeps me from staying in the moment and holding on loosely like you have been telling me, Pablo."

I want to say something, but I can see that I need to wait. I have learned lately that what I think I need to say is probably not going to make much difference.

"Last night, as I thought about all of this, I felt unloved and somehow abandoned, and I began to cry," Stacey continues. "I have been trying to be someone I am not all these years, and now I can see why I get stuck out on the court with my performance blocked so often.

"You know, when I watched *The Last Samurai,* I kinda got it, as I told you back when we spoke after your trip to South Africa to see the kids. Do you remember that?"

"I remember it well, Stacey," I reply.

"Now I not only get it, but suddenly it is becoming clear why I was unable to be in that ideal place. I was always going from control to just giving up."

I feel an amazing amount of compassion for Stacey at this moment, and though I want to speak, I continue to sit silently, giving her all my attention as I look at her and nod to acknowledge what she is saying.

"Well, now let me tell you what I did this morning. After crying for a while and letting go of so many things last night, I knew I had to call home and talk to my dad to tell him how I felt. I was going to call him last night, but I know how tired and grumpy he is normally after a long day at work. So I chose to leave it for this morning, when he would be getting up and feeling refreshed after a night's sleep."

As a coach, I know only too well the possible ramifications of a player extending her wings and starting to fly on her own, breaking away from depending on her parents and family. Yes, I have lost jobs because of this in the past, but there is nothing more precious than watching an individual be set free by the truth, even if it means losing my job because of it.

"I woke up very early this morning and came down stairs and spent some time on my own out here on the balcony," Stacey says. "For the first time in my life, I called on the Higher Power that Terry spoke about last night. It was amazing, Pablo. I sat there and let go of everything, and I mean everything. I told the Higher Power that I was tired of trying so hard. I told Him that letting go was very hard for me because I am a competitor. A wounded one, but nevertheless a competitor.

"I told Him I didn't care what I did for the rest of my life, but I wanted to enjoy it and live in the moment, not worrying so much about what might happen. That I wanted to enjoy the process. I cried again, Pablo, but you know as I cried it felt like this huge weight was being lifted off my shoulders.

"But I also felt like something was calling me a quitter when I did this. It's strange, as you know that quitting is not in my nature and what I am doing is not quitting."

I jump in at this point. "Stacey, just like there is a Higher Power that wants to set your heart free, there is also a lower power that wants to keep you in the jail you have been living in all these years.

"You see, holding on loosely is not about moving to nirvana and living there in the sky floating on the clouds. It's about learning to understand that the results of what we do are not up to us alone. The Higher Power you spoke to this morning loves us and wants the best for us. We must learn to trust that even when things do not go the way we want them to, there is a good reason for this and everything is being done for our ultimate good.

"Like Terry, you will be tempted, when things go wrong or get difficult, to try to regain control. However you know now that you really won't gain control. Instead you will be going back to the place where you have good intentions and pretend to be okay, but in reality you are dying inside and getting nowhere."

"Oh, Pablo, it's so good to hear you say that. I got really worried because I don't want to give up. I just want to be free and be who I am instead of who others expect me to be," Stacey replies, smiling as she continues to recount the morning's events.

"Well, I called my dad. I spoke to him about what I am learning, said I loved him and asked if I could tell him something. I could tell he was somewhat puzzled by my call."

As Stacey says this, my mind wants to rush ahead to come up with all the possible answers I can give her father when he inevitably calls me to ask what's going on. But immediately as I am tempted down this road, I hear God whisper into my heart, "Stay present, Pablo."

"I told my dad a bit of Terry's story and what I had learned from it," Stacy says. "And I told him that it was time I was honest with him about something I have been struggling with all my life.

"I said 'Dad, I am tired of playing tennis trying to win just to make you happy and feel like you love me.' The phone went really quiet on the other end; in fact, it went so quiet that I said 'Hello' a few times before my dad assured me he was still there.

"Now, what he said next is what really amazes me and makes me realize the truth of what Terry shared about dancing, how things aren't always what they seem.

"My dad told me, with a broken voice—I think he was crying, that he was sorry he ever did anything to make me feel this way. He told me he always wanted the best for me. He said this is how his father acted toward him, and that he must have repeated his father's actions without being aware of it. Then he told me that he never felt his dad was pleased with him either. He said that, as he listened to my words, it brought back feelings of sadness about his own relationship with his dad.

"Pablo, I felt so bad for him that I started to cry, too. There we were, my dad and I, crying together on the phone. He told me he was very proud of me and the way I had grown in the last six months. The thing is, Pablo, I didn't even know I was changing in ways he could see, but I guess it's true what you say about our behavior changing when our heart changes."

"You betcha it is, Stacey," I say to her with a growing smile on my face. I am totally blown away by what God is doing, not only in me but also in Stacey and now in her family. This moment reminds me of my time in South Africa with the kids, how they saw a massive change in me because I was relaxing as I realized God loved me, was actually nuts about me. I am amazed at how this one revelation has continued to gain momentum and snowball in my life. And now, like ripples in a pond, it is also affecting those around me.

"At that point, we agreed to hang up and talk again tonight," Stacey continues. "Pablo, could I have been wrong about my dad and what I felt about him?"

"Stacey, as humans we often live on autopilot. Then we realize after it is too late that our behavior, possibly in spite of our good intentions, has actually hurt and maimed those around us. We might have the best intentions in the world, but too often we are attempting to manipulate the lives of others in the same way that we try to manipulate our own. Getting the results and outcome we think we should have becomes our focus; and the sad thing about it is that we don't realize the very outcome we seek is the one that blinds us from life in those moments. We are so busy trying to get something that we miss out on what is being given to us. In your dad's case, he missed out on his relationship with you."

"Pablo, I have one more question," Stacey said. "I am sorry to have so many, but I promise this is the last one for now, as we have to get to practice."

"It's okay, Stacey, you can ask as many questions as you want," I reply. "I can't promise I will have the answer to every one of them or even the answer you might like, but if you are okay with that then go ahead and ask."

"Is this Higher Power God?" Stacey asks.

"Who do you want it to be, Stacey?" I reply.

"I wish it was Someone whom I could talk to and hear. I wish it would be like this amazing Being who is very powerful and strong, but yet playful and loving enough that I can spend time with Him and be who I am without having to pretend to be someone I am not. I wish He was like the perfect Dad we all want and need, I guess."

"Well, Stacey, why don't you ask Him to reveal who He is to you? This way you will discover who He is, and as you do He will be your God and not someone else's," I say to her, amazed by my own words. In the past I would have bulldozed her with the gospel of repentance and baptism, yet now I am comfortable enough to know God is more than able to handle this on His own and bring Stacey into His family if this is the right time for her. I can see Stacey is blown away by my answer, giving me great hope and faith that she will seek Him in her own time.

She has tasted Him without even knowing it, and what she has tasted so far is very good.

As we get up from the table, we agree to meet downstairs in half an hour to catch the shuttle to the site where we will practice. I get into the elevator to return to the room, and I can't help but stand there in amazement.

This is just incredible. I can hardly believe what is happening in me and around me. It's like a dream come true. In fact, it's much better than any dream I could have put together myself.

As I exit the elevator, I smile as I sense God tell me, "The best is yet to come."

It's 11 a.m., and we enter the practice court with our training partner and her coach. The girls get out their rackets and begin to hit in the service boxes. It has turned out to be a glorious day of sunshine. The temperature is rapidly approaching 90 degrees, and the wind is virtually still. There are people all around the court to watch the girls practice, and I can hear cameras clicking away.

As I walk by Stacey on my way to pick up a ball in the corner, she turns around and says, "I feel so light and free, Pablo. It's amazing."

"I know what you mean, and guess what?" I say, with a great big smile.

"What?" she asks.

"The best is yet to come."

After the girls have hit for a while, we stop to drink some water, Stacey's practice partner turns to her and asks, "Hey Stacey, what are you so happy about?"

Stacey turns to me and starts to laugh uncontrollably. The other player and her coach look at me in disbelief as they don't understand why she is laughing. As she calms down, she gives her practice partner a great look of happy mischief and replies. "I could tell you, but you wouldn't believe it. So let's just say I am no longer carrying around excess baggage."

"Whatever it is, I want some of it," the other coach says.

"When I figure it all out, you will be the first one to know— though it might be a long while before that happens," Stacey responds, still laughing.

As I watch Stacey play a set, I realize she is playing with an amazing new freedom. She displays the kind of aggression I have been trying to coach her toward since I met her. But up until now I've had somewhat limited success. With all that has happened yesterday and this morning, here is the result I've been hoping for. *Wow, maybe God is right and the best IS yet to come.*

After practice, I pick up my cell phone from the small court-side table and see that I have a text from Terry. It says his meetings have gone longer than expected, but he will be available to join us for dinner tonight if that's okay with us.

"Stacey, are you okay if Terry joins us for dinner tonight?" I ask, before replying to the message.

"Heck yeah, Pablo," she replies with a big smile on her face.

"Is 7:30 okay with you?" I ask.

132

"Yes, that's fine," she replies as she is signing autographs for the fans who have watched her practice.

I reply to Terry's text, confirming that we will meet him in the hotel lobby at 7:30 p.m. Then I walk to the referee's office to see who and when we play tomorrow.

"Stacey, we play third from 10 a.m. on center court," I tell her, looking at the draw. Unfortunately, we don't have the best of draws, but I choose to remain in the moment and not worry about the results. We have done our work to the best of our abilities; the rest is in God's hands.

We grab something to eat for lunch before one last afternoon practice. Once again I see Stacey playing some scintillating tennis. I can't help but feel excited about the week, yet I keep myself in the moment, holding on loosely to all that is going on in us and around us.

It's amazing how much faith and positive energy I feel inside even though the draw suggests I should be feeling totally different. This has been a great day, not for tennis reasons so much as for what has happened inside Stacey and me.

As we arrive back at the hotel, we head to our rooms to get ready for dinner. We will meet Terry in a few hours. As Stacey leaves the elevator she turns to me with a smile on her face and says, "I am going to call my dad before we go for dinner, and guess what? I am not scared about it."

I smile back at her with mixed feelings of gratitude and the kind of pride a father feels for his own daughter. "I am so proud of you, Stace."

As the elevator doors close, I whisper a prayer for her as I know the next hour or so is very important. I am too aware that the lower power is anxious to screw things up when we least expect it. Still, I remind myself to stay in the moment and trust the Higher One who is responsible for starting this good work in Stacey.

The clock hits 7:25 p.m. as I enter the elevator once again, heading for the lobby where I will meet Stacey and Terry. As the elevator doors open, I see the two of them talking away.

"Hello Terry, how are you mate?" I say as I walk toward them and embrace Terry with a big hug.

"I am very well, Pablo. Thanks! How was your day?" he replies.

"It was great, mate. We had a fantastic time together this morning over breakfast," I say.

"Yes, Stacey was just telling me all about it. It is fantastic, isn't it?" he says.

"It sure is, Ter," I reply as we leave the hotel to find the car that will take us to the restaurant.

"I have chosen a nice Argentinean restaurant for us. Is that okay with you, Ter?" I ask as we get into the car.

"Oh yes, Pablo, you know I love that wonderful meat from your country," he replies.

"Great! So Argentinean it is," I say to the driver, giving him directions to the restaurant where I dined several times when I was in this city three years earlier.

It is a beautiful evening. The sun is still up, and that wonderful, cool breeze from the morning has returned. I am sitting in the front seat of the car, and Terry and Stacey are together in the back talking away like last night. I can't help but overhear their conversation, but I choose to talk with the driver during the short trip as I realize that minding my own business would be most useful at this time.

When we arrive at the restaurant, we get out of the car and, like last night, laugh together as the driver asks what time he should pick us up for the return trip. "Don't worry, we will catch a cab again tonight. Thank you very much for the ride," I say, closing the car door.

Climbing the stairs to the second-floor restaurant, I have flashbacks of my home country when I smell the beef cooking on the barbecue. The waiter greets us at the door and takes us to our table; we sit down and start to look over the menus.

"Talk about staying in the moment. Read this selection of meat," I say as both Terry and Stacey laugh.

"What do you recommend, Pablo?" asks Terry.

"I recommend the *bife de chorizo*, cooked medium, with a nice salad," I reply.

"Okay, so it is," Terry replies with a great big smile.

Stacey orders the same, cooked well done.

"I was telling Terry that I called my dad this morning and was about to tell him about my call tonight when we got here," Stacey says, as Terry and I look at each other, realizing how huge this moment is for Stacey.

"Okay, do you want to share that with us now or after dinner?" I ask.

Stacey thinks for a bit and says, "I'd rather wait until after dinner as I want to be fully present when they bring my steak."

CHAPTER 9

REALITY CHECK

I admit I once lived by rumors of you;
now I have it all firsthand—from my own eyes and ears!
I'm sorry—forgive me. I'll never do that again, I promise!
I'll never again live on crusts of hearsay, crumbs of rumor.

—Job 42:5-6

As our meal winds down, I ask the waiter if the restaurant serves *mate*, an Argentinean herb we drink back home at the end of a meal. It is usually served in a cup made from a pumpkin-like material and with a metal straw; a gold-plated tip on the straw becomes hot, which kills germs from our mouth. The herb can also be prepared as a tea known as *mate cocido*.

In my book, no Argentinean meal is complete without a *mate*, and, with Stacey getting ready to tell us about her call home, I think sipping away at a *mate* would be ideal while we listen to her.

Much to my surprise, the waiter answers positively. "Would you like one?" he replies.

"Stacey, Terry, would you guys like one?" I ask, knowing Stacey doesn't because she has already tried *mate* and hated it.

"Is that the drink I had from Argentina?" she asks, screwing up her face.

"Yes, that's the one," I reply.

"Then I really don't want one. In fact, I am happy to just keep drinking my water," she says.

I look over at Terry, and of course he wants one. So I order two.

"Guys, I want to tell you about my call home tonight as it sprung a few surprises on me, and I am sure both of you will like them," Stacey says.

"Okay, Stacey. Go ahead; we are all ears," I reply.

"I phoned home when I arrived back at my room after we said goodbye, and the first surprise was that I wasn't afraid like

I have always been when calling home in the past. This fear had become such a part of me that I was not even aware of it, but today when I started dialing the numbers I noticed a big difference. I felt calm; the fear was no longer there."

Both Terry and I nod in approval and tell her that this is great to hear.

"My mom answered the phone, as my dad was not home. She and I talked for a bit, then she asked me in a strange voice, 'What did you say to your dad this morning when you guys spoke on the phone?' Naturally I replied, 'Why are you asking me that, mom?'"

"She said, 'As you know very well, your dad never calls home unless he needs something or there is an urgent matter that needs taking care of,' she replied. 'Today, he called me three times between leaving home and a few hours ago. The strange thing was that he called just to see how I was and ask if I needed anything. I obviously loved it, but it felt very strange. So I thought it might have something to do with the chat the two of you had this morning.'

"I told my mom in a roundabout way what my dad and I had spoken about. I was really uncomfortable telling her exactly what we said. The matter is very much between me and my dad, and I didn't know if my dad wanted her to know about it," Stacey explains.

"Could it be possible that he called home like that because of the talk he and I had this morning?" Stacey asks, looking at Terry and I as the waiter arrives with our drinks.

"Terry, do you want to answer that?" I ask, as I begin to sip away at my hot drink.

"Sure, no problem," Terry replies.

"Stacey, when we have a reality check, it is common for us to try to quickly fix the situation by changing our behavior. We fall into the trap of thinking that changing the way we behave will solve the problem," Terry says.

"The trouble with this approach is that the behavior we are trying to change is actually only a symptom of what is really wrong. We may be able to change our behavior, temporarily anyway, but the real problem is a condition of our heart. In my case, the problem was my need for approval and, similarly to mine, yours was the need to see your father smile. Of course I allowed my heart condition to continue much longer and do much more damage than you have.

"The only real change that will stand the test of time and bring healing and lasting change in our behavior can be made by submitting ourselves to the Higher Power and living in surrender, or as Pablo says, 'holding on loosely.'

"This way we will not be so hard on ourselves every time we make a mistake. We will be able to realize we are on a journey, and as you know, journeys take time. We will also be released from trying to manipulate the outcome and the results, and instead we will be able to enjoy the process of allowing the Higher Power to change us in His time and in His way."

"Okay, I get why he did that then," Stacey replies. "Wow! That's amazing. I never thought of it like this."

"Another good example is when Pablo attempts to change something in your game. If he is a good coach, he will understand and explain to you that the change will take some time. When you know you have time and you don't need to get it right by next week's tournament, then you are able to relax and stop being afraid to make mistakes as you are developing a new technique or shot," Terry says. Turning to me, he asks, "Am I right in saying that, Pablo?"

"Yes, you're right, and I think it is very much the way Stacey and I try to work together," I reply.

"The great thing about this approach is that the two of you are actually involved in the journey together, and you learn and see new things along the way," Terry says. "It's like a school field trip where you interact with the teacher as you visit and learn about a new place. Learning in this way means that you actually discover new truth for yourself; and by understanding how you arrived at this truth, you can help others reach this place in the future," Terry says.

"That's awesome!" Stacey replies, smiling. "So I need to tell my dad about this then."

"Well, I would wait until you see him to do that," Terry says. "I think the important thing now is to forgive him for what he is not able to do and love him for who he is. Go after and love his heart. That's the way the Higher Power loves us. He doesn't look for a certain behavior, but instead He loves our hearts and fills us with this love that transforms us as He heals us from the inside out. The Higher Power does not rush His healing; He knows this is a journey. He knows what our hearts need, and He has the power and ability to provide it. We, on the other hand, want to change ourselves as quickly as possible because we feel uncomfortable or ashamed of our weaknesses. The Higher Power has seen it all before, and He knows that gradual change is much more likely to last."

"Did you manage to talk to your dad later? Did he make it back home in time?" I ask Stacey.

"Oh yes, I spoke to him. He arrived home while I was on the phone with my mom," she replies. "And it was amazing. Even his voice was different than before. I could tell something had happened. We spoke about many things, and at the end, he wished me luck for my match tomorrow. He didn't give me the usual chatter about what I should remember and what I should or should not do. It was a great conversation."

As she finishes saying this, I whisper a prayer of thanksgiving to God, as this could have gone in a totally different direction.

"That's great, Stacey! We are so happy for you," I reply, noticing that Terry's smile is as big as mine.

"The important thing now, Stacey, is that you take one day at a time in your relationship with your dad. It sounds like your conversation with him hit a sore spot in his heart, hence the behavior change you noticed. Remember that this behavior can change again suddenly, and it often does," Terry says.

"The important thing is that you know what is really going on when this happens. It is the wound inside and not your dad himself talking. Understanding this will help you love him, and it is not always easy to love those who hurt us with their actions, especially those closest to us."

"I will remember that," Stacey replies with a more serious face. "My dad can be quite nasty sometimes."

"Pablo, do you want to add anything else? I want to try this *mate* before it gets cold," Terry says.

"I think enough has been said," I reply. I would like to talk about tomorrow's match but I feel Stacey has enough to process right now.

We're practically the last people in the restaurant now, though it isn't that late. I ask for the bill and pay it as Terry finishes his drink, then we go outside to catch a cab.

"Thank you for allowing me the privilege to be a part of your journey," Terry says looking Stacey straight in the eyes.

"And you, young man, thank you for dinner, and once again thank you for giving me a second chance," he says to me as we embrace.

"It is my privilege and joy to be your friend, Terry," I reply.

"I will be there tomorrow to watch you, Stacey," Terry tells her as he gets into his cab.

On the way back to the hotel, I can tell that something is troubling Stacey. I choose to let her tell me on her own instead of trying to pull it out of her. I turn to look out the window at the coastline, and she asks, "Pablo, you know this Higher Power keeps coming up. Both you and Terry talk about it and I want to know who or what it is."

I really don't want to blow this moment by saying the wrong thing, so I shoot a prayer arrow to God. *Please help me.* Everything inside me wants to share the gospel with her, but for some reason I don't feel it's the right thing to do.

"Did you ask the Higher Power to reveal itself to you?" I ask her.

"Well yes, kind of, this morning when I spoke to it outside of the hotel," she replies.

"Okay, then give Him a chance and I am sure He will," I reply. "I think you will agree He is certainly showing you many new things; it is important for you to remember that this is a journey. Don't rush things. Allow things to come into your life as they will. Enjoy the process and believe me when I tell you that He has heard you calling and He will answer when you least expect it."

Stacey turns to look out the window at the beautiful coastline we can see from the road, and we spend the rest of the journey to the hotel in silence.

"You did great tonight, Stacey," I tell her as we say good night.

"Thanks, Pablo. I am so grateful to both you and Terry for all you are doing. No one else has gone this far to help me before. I guess that's why you are good at what you do," Stacey replies.

"Stacey, I do this because someone did it for me many years ago. I do it because I care for you. I see you first as an individual and a friend and then as the player I coach," I say.

As we embrace I say, "Good night, sleep well, champ! See you at nine for breakfast."

"Yep. You too. See you then," Stacey replies.

"Look what my dad sent me, Pablo!" Stacey says, showing me a text message on her phone. It says that he loves her no matter what happens in her game today.

"That's great, Stacey. I am very pleased to see that," I answer, knowing it's her dad's response to the phone conversation he and I had last night after I got back to my room. Stacey is not aware that the two of us talked, and I think it is better to keep it that way for now.

Our conversation was a short one, but it was very relevant. During the many months I've been trying to communicate these things to Stacey's dad, I have always been met with distrust. It's as if he suspected I was trying to manipulate their family, which was the last thing on my mind. Her dad is especially possessive of her, which I can understand, being a dad myself. But it was his unwillingness to let her go that was actually stalling her career. And I know his heart's desire is for her to succeed. He couldn't see that what he was doing was actually standing in the way of the very thing he hoped for.

Last night for the first time, I could tell his heart was open and he had finally begun to see the truth I had been speaking of all this time. But his change of heart is not the direct result of anything I've done; it was the change he saw in Stacey that brought about his new perspective.

I can hardly believe all this is happening. And to think that it started with a reality check of my own in an airplane restroom all that time ago, followed by an encounter with a juggler in the airport. Wow! It's amazing what happens when we just hold on loosely and trust God to do what He has always said He would do.

It's match day, and it's very hot. Swarms of people are everywhere. The smell of the hot dogs and hamburgers grilling at the food stands fills the air along the sidewalks surrounding the clubhouse. There is virtually no wind, which is amazing considering the forecast for gale force winds most of the week.

After the warm up, we find a quiet place to talk, as we always do, about the match and how Stacey should play tactically against the day's opponent. We find a spot under a nice big tree in a location the crowd can't access so that we can talk without distractions. Nevertheless, the crowd shouts out to Stacey. "Just wave at them Stacey, so they are happy and we can get on with this," I say.

With a huge smile, Stacey turns around, waves and blows the fans a kiss, which causes an eruption of cheers.

Normally we would discuss tactics for the game, but today my inclination is to encourage her to focus on hitting the ball as freely as she has the last two days.

"How are you feeling, Stacey," I ask.

"I feel great, Pablo. I know I have a very tough match today. But, you know, I am going to stay in the moment the way I have done in all the practices since arriving here," she replies.

"That's great, Stacey. That's exactly what I was going to encourage you to do. We know this girl well, so you know what you need to do tennis-wise," I reply. "There is just one thing I would like to share with you before you go get ready for the match. When you are out there and you are in the moment, be aware that it will feel very strange."

Stacey starts to laugh.

"Why are you laughing?" I inquire.

"These last two days have rewritten the meaning of the word *strange*, Pablo."

"Yes, I know what you mean. But isn't it great, all that has happened in such a short period of time?"

"Yes, it is fantastic, and I would not have it any other way," she replies with a great big smile.

"Okay, back to what I was saying earlier. It will feel very strange to stay in the moment. This is perfectly normal. Whatever you do, don't start to get upset with yourself if you lose that place at some point. It is important for you to realize that you are there to enjoy the process, and the results will come when they are supposed to," I say.

Stacey agrees to keep her focus in the moment as best she can, and we get up to walk back to the clubhouse. As we do, I hear Terry call my name from the other side of the fence.

"Okay, Stacey, I will meet you at the referees' desk just before the match," I tell her as she heads to the locker room and I acknowledge Terry.

Stacey greets Terry with a wave and a big smile. "Hi, Terry," she calls out.

"Hey, Stacey," Terry replies, also smiling broadly.

"Will you please let him in?" I ask the guard, who begins acting in a strange, obnoxious manner toward me with no apparent reason. "I am sorry, but he has a pass and is allowed to come in this way," I add.

Terry works his way to the front of the crowd, and the guard has no choice but to let him in.

"Thank you very much," I say to the guard.

"You handled that very well, Pablo," Terry says, as the way I mishandled the check-in attendant back at the airport some time ago flashes through my mind.

"You know, Terry, you are right, my friend. In the past, I would have blown up and told that guy where to go, yet I had no desire to do that today," I reply with a smile. "God is good, my friend."

"He sure is, Pablo."

"Where are you with all that, Terry?" I ask him as we walk towards the clubhouse. You see, being raised in a so-called Christian home that was more like the home of a heavenly policeman, Terry grew up thinking God was strictly interested in his behavior. He believed that if he messed up, God would not want anything to do with him. This led him to hide things from his parents and to try hiding things from God, even though that's impossible to do. He learned to fight his own battles and hide problems, hoping he would stay in the good graces of his parents and of God. Knowing all of this, I am not sure where he stands with God now.

"Well Pablo, a few years back I met a group of guys who called themselves believers and followers of Christ, but not Christians," Terry replies. "These guys met together in one of their homes twice a week. They were real with one another; they didn't pretend to be something they were not or act in a particular way because they were 'Christian.' They had real relationships with each other, and I could see the love and life of God in them in a way I had never experienced in a more formal church setting. It drew me in; I began to meet with them, and since then I have never looked back.

"Even if I don't meet with them for a couple of weeks because of work or if I can't read my Bible as often as I'd like to, I don't feel guilty and full of condemnation. It's amazing," he says. "My relationship with God does not depend on those meetings, my relationships with the other guys, or even what I do or don't do. It is between me and Him. Everything else is a bonus."

I'm thrilled to learn this. But I can hear Stacey's match being called over the loudspeaker, so I work my way down to the referees' desk to meet up with her just before she goes on the court. Terry is beside me, keeping quiet and very low-key. What a difference from the guy I knew all those years ago.

"Godspeed, Stacey," I tell her as we high-five each other.

The match is on center court today. I have a microphone fitted in case Stacey calls me into the court in one of the changeovers for some advice. "Just say something for me, please," says the TV audio guy.

"Life's great, and I love my friend Terry," I say into the microphone.

The man smiles and so does Terry. "Okay, fine. It's working. You know what to do, right?" he asks.

"Yeah, sure. Don't worry," I reply.

As we begin to walk away from the clubhouse, we hear someone call out to Terry in a strong voice.

We turn around, and Terry shouts, "Gary!"

It's Terry's friend from years ago at the club. He is the guy Terry credits with helping him recover from his addictions. He's now working with a TV network broadcasting the match.

They embrace for a few seconds. I am getting a bit anxious to be in the court when Stacey goes in, but I choose to wait a bit before saying anything.

"When I heard this young man say 'my friend Terry,' I looked at the camera monitor in the clubhouse. Sure enough, it was you," Gary says.

"What are you doing these days?" Terry asks, as they have lost touch recently.

"I am working for a TV network, helping them set things up," Gary replies.

"You look great," Terry tells him. "And it is so good to see you again. This is my friend Pablo."

"Nice to meet you, Pablo. And yes, it is nice to see you too, Terry, and see you are still doing well. You haven't forgotten who you are, right?" Gary asks.

"No I haven't," Terry says with a smile.

As I stand there and watch them talk, I am amazed at the powerful moment I am experiencing. If it weren't for Gary, this moment would not be happening, yet here we are. I am filled with a mix of emotions that is hard to describe, an overwhelming passion and happiness in response to the evidence of God's hand in what happened between those two.

How many times we miss God because we expect things to happen within a religious box we've created in our own minds. And how often the same box keeps us from what God can do and wants to do in us and through us.

"Gents, I am sorry to interrupt, but I have to get into the stadium as the girls are about to go in," I say.

"Yep. Sure," Terry replies.

The guys embrace again and agree to talk later. "Nice to meet you Pablo, and good luck," Gary says.

"Yes, it's great to meet you too, Gary. And thanks for what you did for Terry," I reply.

"No sweat," he says, walking back to the TV trailer.

Terry and I walk into the stadium, and there isn't an empty seat in the house. The crowd is full of expectation for the match. The announcer introduces the girls, and one by one they come onto the court to a huge ovation from the crowd. It is still very sunny, with virtually no wind. Terry and I take our seats as automatic cameras click rapidly, photographing the girls.

As the match begins, I can tell that Stacey is doing very well at staying present. She plays an unbelievable first game and breaks her opponent's serve. Then she holds her own and stays in command for the remainder of the set. Terry and I encourage her from the stands. I am amazed at how little she is looking at me today. Normally she would fix her eyes on me after every point; today, apart from two occasions, she is keeping to herself, which thrills me to see.

With the second set, her opponent picks up her game and they reach four–all. This is a good moment to see how Stacey reacts, as situations like this would typically cause her to jam up. Today she manages to play some very solid tennis in this hard spot. At a key point, she produces an amazing winning shot to take the game and then serve for the match. The fans are on their feet; they recognize this as a surprising breakthrough.

But I see it differently, for I am beginning to understand this is the kind of power produced by holding on loosely and staying in the moment rather than worrying about results.

Stacey waves to the crowd, and after doing an interview with the camera crew, she meets us outside the stadium by the clubhouse. "Come on! That was a sterling performance," I say, embracing Stacey. Terry congratulates her as well.

"Stacey, you have press at five o'clock. Is that okay?" the WTA press officer asks her. Stacey nods while looking at me for approval. It works for me as it gives her plenty of time to cool down, stretch and eat something.

Terry leaves us to go chat more with Gary so Stacey and I can debrief from the match without feeling we are leaving him out.

"So how was it, Stacey?" I ask her intrigued, especially anticipating what she will say regarding the second set.

"Pablo, it was amazing. I felt so at peace out there. I didn't even notice the crowd was there today," she said. "I felt so still; when we came to four, all in the second set, I didn't even think about the score or jump ahead to plan my next move. I just played one ball at a time."

"That's fantastic, Stacey!" I reply.

"You know, when I am in this place, I feel like I can do just about anything," she continues. "I hope you don't mind that I didn't really look at you, but I didn't feel the need to. It was almost as if I was okay on my own."

"Not a problem at all. In fact, I am very happy to hear that," I reply, knowing most coaches would be threatened by words like this. In their insecurity, they would expect the player to move on and leave them behind, meaning they'd lose their job.

As Stacey cools down on the bike in the gym, I think of all the players and people in life in general who never tap their full potential. So often, those they look to for guidance are keeping them in a box so that they never reach the point of independence. *Insecure coaches and leaders are one of the biggest potential-killers in the world,* I am thinking as Terry walks into the gym.

"Okay, Stacey, get a shower and we will meet you downstairs by the lounge when you're ready," I tell her as we leave the gym.

"How was the chat with Gary?" I ask Terry.

"It was great to see him again. Unfortunately he is leaving after this next match for another job, so we can't get together tonight as I would have liked to," Terry replies.

As we sit down on the couches outside the lounge, I whisper thanks to God for all He has been doing in us and for us and, of course, for helping Stacey today.

"The best is yet to come, Pablo," I hear him say again as I stare out into the sponsors' area. Little did I realize exactly how much better things were about to become.

CHAPTER 10

THE FINAL STRETCH

"Then he isn't safe?" said Lucy.

"Safe?" said Mr. Beaver; "don't you hear what Mrs. Beaver tells you? Who said anything about safe? 'Course he isn't safe. But he's good. He's the King, I tell you."

—The Lion, The Witch, and the Wardrobe

Who can it be this early? I think as my hotel room phone rings.

"Hello," I say with a deep voice, the product of being half asleep. The room is dark, and I am nicely tucked into bed.

"Pablo!" the voice shouts from the other side of the phone.

"Dad?" I answer, recognizing the voice of my father but puzzled as to what he is doing here.

"Yes, it's me. I'm here in the lobby; come down," he replies.

"No, Dad, you can come up to my room. It's 512, and I am still in bed," I reply.

"Okay, I am coming up," he says.

I hang up the phone and go to the bathroom, stumbling against the door as I have forgotten to turn on the light on my way in. *I can't believe he is here,* I think as I rush through my morning routine.

As I flush the toilet, I hear the knock on the door.

"Hey Dad!" I say as we embrace for a few seconds. I haven't seen him in more than a year, so though it is extremely early in the morning this is a special moment I enjoy whenever it happens. Every part of me wishes our visits were more frequent, but they have been years apart since I was 13 and sent to a tennis academy away from home. It was my father's dream for me to become a top professional tennis player, but it never happened.

"How is it going, Pablo?" he asks.

"It's going very well. But tell me, what are you doing here?" I ask.

"Well, I am in town on business, and I saw on the WTA site that you guys were here, so I thought I would stop and give you a surprise," he replies.

"Oh, I see. Well, that's very nice of you," I say.

"What is going on today?" he asks.

"Stacey is playing third in the main court, where the matches start at one o'clock. I am meeting her for breakfast in two hours," I reply. "A friend of mine named Terry is here, but he is not staying with us. He will be meeting us at the club, as he has business to take care of before he comes to watch Stacey. Dad, you don't mind if I get a bit more sleep do you?" I ask.

"No, not at all. In fact, I will take advantage of this other bed, if that's okay with you," he replies. "I didn't sleep very well on the flight last night."

As I lean back on my pillow and turn off the lights, I whisper a prayer of thanks to God. Amazing things happen when I hold on loosely. In all the years I have longed for my father to just drop in on me like he has just done, it never happened. Yet here he is when I least expect it.

Living in this place of surrender generates an amazing power. As we welcome mystery into our lives, we leave room for God to do the good things He wants to do. There is a very big difference between living life full of expectations and living expectantly.

The first almost always ends in disappointment, leaving you wanting. If you continue down this road, frustration develops, which leads to unresolved anger, which, if not dealt with, results in a bitterness inside that will kill you.

Living expectantly, on the other hand, is rooted in hope and faith and grounded in the love of a God who has amazing things to give us. This generous God delights in blessing us with His gifts when the time is right and we are ready for them. As if this wasn't enough, the most beautiful thing about this life is that nothing that happens can change this reality. The love of this amazing God never changes, regardless of circumstances. If a blessing doesn't happen on a certain day, it doesn't mean it never will; it means it was not for today.

"Hello," I answer again with a half-asleep voice.

"This is your wake-up call, sir!" the very cheerful voice says from the other end of the phone.

"Okay, thanks," I reply. "Come on, Dad. It's time to get up," I say to my father before I jump in the shower to prepare to meet Stacey for breakfast.

A short time later, he and I head out of the room to make our way downstairs. "You got the key, Pablo?" he asks.

As we exit the elevator, Stacey is already standing outside the breakfast area. She and my father have met on previous occasions, so they greet one another and immediately embrace.

"Did you know he was coming, Pablo?" Stacey asks.

"No, I didn't. It was a mixed surprise this morning when my phone rang."

"What do you mean *mixed*?" Dad asks.

"Well, Dad, it was six a.m. when you showed up, and you know how much I like my sleep these days," I reply smiling, as both he and Stacey laugh.

As we work our way to the table, I notice the restaurant is quite busy. Many fans from out of town stay in this hotel during tournaments in hopes of spotting the players. The fans are out in force this morning, so the hostess shows us to one of the last tables in the back.

"I feel great this morning, Pablo," Stacey says. "I had a good chat with my parents last night. It was completely relaxed. My dad was a bit grumpy because of something that happened at work, but we still had a great conversation."

"That's great, Stacey," I say, affirming the positive communication with her parents.

As we wrap up our breakfast, a fan approaches the table to ask for an autograph. While Stacey obliges, my father inquires, "What's happened to you two?"

"What do you mean?" I ask.

"Well, you two seem to be so ... in harmony. I don't know how to describe it. It's really weird," he says.

I smile as Stacey sits down again, and I tell him in Spanish, *Despues te cuento*, which means, *I will tell you later*.

The remainder of the morning goes smoothly. As my dad and I wait outside the locker room for Stacey, someone taps my shoulder from behind me.

"Hey, Pablo. How are you, mate?"

"Terry! I am very well. Look who is here," I reply, pointing to my father.

"Hello, sir, how are you doing?" he asks my dad.

"I am very well, Terry. You look great," my dad replies.

When Stacey comes out of the locker room, we wish her Godspeed for the match, then work our way down to the stands.

We're watching this match from the same place we watched the last one, and I have been wired for the match once again, so I must be careful what I say. The stadium is packed with people as before, and it is another hot day with very little wind.

Stacey comes out and plays a great match. She beats her opponent in a little more than an hour, an impressive rate; but even more impressive is the way she moves on the court.

"Wow, she has really improved, Pablo," my father says.

"You think so, Dad?" I ask.

"Yes, she is playing much better than when I last saw her, and she is very calm on the court," he replies.

"She must have a great coach," Terry says, as he winks and smiles at my dad.

"Yes, of course," my father replies with that proud look only a father can have.

As the tournament continues, Stacey finds herself in the final, where she will play an opponent inside the world's top players whom she has never defeated.

I have a few hours alone before we will all have dinner. Dad has gone shopping at the massive shopping center next door. I want to spend this time with God.

Staying in the moment these days is becoming almost second nature to me, so I am happy to just sit silently waiting for God to speak. In the past I, would have started talking right away, not that there is anything wrong with that exactly. But I realize that being content to wait silently while keeping my mind focused on the present moment rather than fast-forwarding to the future or rewinding to the past is a significant change in me. It is so good to lie down with no pressure to say or do something to get God's attention, knowing that He is mindful of me at all times in all circumstances.

During this quiet time, I sense my heart overflowing with gratitude to God. Strangely, even though I am not saying or hearing anything, I feel His pleasure. I sense He is here with me, and we are enjoying each other's company without using any words. I stay in this place for some time, simply delighting in the presence of my heavenly Dad.

The significance of times like this is amazing. I don't feel anything specifically, but I realize the differences in my attitude and in my reactions to certain situations. God is making miraculous changes in me apart from any conscious effort of my own.

My quiet time of reflection comes to an end as I hear the key click in the door.

"Look at these shirts I found on sale," Dad says, pulling them out one by one from the different bags.

"Wow, Dad. Those are nice," I reply.

"Do you really like them?" he asks, beginning to try on one of them.

"Yes, I really do. The colors suit you very well."

My father will be leaving in a few hours, so I plan to spend the rest of our time together talking and sharing what has been going on in our lives in the months since our last visit. While he showers, I close my eyes and return to that peaceful place in my mind where I was before he came in.

In the past, I would have thought the interruption had quenched the Spirit, and I would have shied away from returning. These days I am coming to understand that God is much more relaxed than I even dared to imagine. *What a beautiful thing!* With no expectation that I control every circumstance in my life or even in my prayer life, He holds on as loosely as He encourages me to do.

After my dad exits the shower, dresses and is ready to talk, I take him by the shoulders and look straight into his eyes. "I love you, Dad, and I am very glad that we can share this time together," I tell him, knowing full well he has not been the perfect dad, though he has tried in his own way.

As his eyes tear up, we embrace, and he replies, "Thanks, Pablo. Thanks so much for saying that. I am so proud of you, Pablo. You have achieved so much, and look at you! You have changed so much, it is amazing. You deserve a medal."

I simply smile and quietly thank the One who is worthy of all the medals that have ever existed.

"Pablo, when are you going to come see me?" he asks, continuing.

"I am not sure, Dad. You know I travel quite a bit, and I don't want to promise what I cannot deliver," I reply.

"I know that feeling well, son," he says, turning to look at me. His look tells me he regrets the many family times he missed because work and other things took priority. What he thought would provide freedom to spend time at home in reality took away that very freedom. What he thought those things would give, they actually robbed from him as he became busier and less available.

"I know what you are feeling, Dad," I say. "I know the feeling very well. I know how painful it is to wake up every morning in a different place than the ones you love."

Dad remains silent.

Suddenly the room closes up. Here we are, two people a generation apart affected by the same wound, the same flaws, but with one huge difference. One of us knows the forgiveness, the healing and the freedom of a real relationship with God; the other doesn't. I sit there longing to share this with my dad, but I sense the time is not right.

He finishes packing, and I accompany him downstairs to catch the hotel's airport shuttle. The awkward silence in the elevator provides all the evidence I need that we both know these parting moments all too well, and we hate that it is time to say good-bye again.

"Bye, Dad," I say as we embrace with a hardy hug.

"Bye, Pablo, and thank you," he replies.

I notice tears in his eyes, and I don't dare to elaborate on this heartfelt moment as I am fighting back tears in my own red eyes.

I watch the shuttle pull away, remembering my dad's countless departures throughout my life, then return to my room. I can't hold back the tears any longer. But as they flow freely, I notice something different about these tears than those that have followed previous good-byes with my dad. I feel like the issues and anger toward my father have been lifted out of me.

Oh God, please help me, I call out sobbing. Although I don't hear anything in response, I sense a strong presence within me. I sense the arms of God holding me as I cry myself to sleep.

Waking the next day, I lie in my bed for a while reflecting on what happened last night. I feel lighter and more free inside, but when I get out of bed and look in the mirror, I can see my eyes are bloodshot from crying. After showering, I pour half a bottle of Visine into my eyes. I am not embarrassed like I used to be when people can tell I've been crying, but today I do not want anything to distract Stacey from her big match.

At breakfast with both Stacey and Terry, I make every effort to appear as fresh and calm as possible. It's not much of a struggle, as I honestly feel amazing inside. I feel new and free, like another part of me has come alive. I sense a surge of energy throughout my body as I sit there; what a powerful impact holding on loosely has in our lives as we learn to understand it and become more comfortable living it.

As we warm up, I can tell that Stacey is feeling nervous. Today's match is a big one; the stakes are very high. As we sit down to chat, she admits, "I am a bit nervous today, Pablo."

"You would not be human if you were not nervous, Stacey," I reassure her. "It's okay to be nervous, just as it's okay to be afraid. The important thing is to work with these feelings rather than pretend you don't feel them. Stay present, and hold on loosely. Don't think too much about what is happening; enjoy every moment, trusting that whatever you do will be good enough, and let things happen as they will."

"Thanks," she says, agreeing. "I already feel much better after telling you about it." We talk another minute or two about the match, then she is on her way to the locker room.

"How is she, Pablo?" Terry asks.

"You know, Ter, I think she is going to be fine today," I respond with great peace inside, knowing we are on the brink of something great.

Terry and I take our seats in the stands. Once again the place is packed, and the temperature is very warm, though today there is a gentle breeze. The announcer welcomes everyone, thanks all the sponsors then introduces the players.

As the ladies begin the match, I feel my heart beating expectantly—exciting possibilities are open to us today. Still, there are no guarantees, so I calm myself and focus on the moment. Over the usual crowd noise, I hear the soft wind, birds chirping, Terry breathing next to me—things I normally wouldn't hear. This is evidence of the incredible stillness inside me, and my prayer is that Stacey is experiencing the same peace.

The match begins, and our opponent shows signs of her dominant status from the start. Before long Stacey is down 5–2 and calls me into the court during the changeover. Arriving at the chair, I sense that all is not well with her.

"What's happening, Stacey?" I ask, allowing her room to tell me what is going on.

"Pablo, my mind is running away from me. All I can think of is winning the match and what it will mean to me as a player if I win," she replies.

"Stacey, look at me," I say. She fixes her eyes on me as sweat pours down her forehead. "The answer to this is inside you. You are focusing on the wrong things instead of looking inside. Play one point at a time, and stop trying to control the outcome. I want you to look at me after every point until you have calmed down and feel peace inside."

"Okay, I will," she says.

"Come on! You can do this," I say. "This is your day. Go out there and enjoy the moment!" Then I get up and run out of the court and back to my seat.

Stacey comes out and plays a much better game but loses the set. Nevertheless, I sense there has been a breakthrough and things will change in the next set.

Sure enough, Stacey begins the next set very well. I can see in her eyes that she is now flowing in the stillness she had in her recent matches. As the set progresses, she glances at me less often; she wins the second set.

Now in the third set, we reach four–all, and Stacey has a break point on her opponent's serve. As our challenger gets the balls from the ball girl to serve, the crowd is shouting "Come on, Stacey! You can do this!" The chair umpire asks for silence as the player is ready to serve. Immediately the whole stadium falls silent. I can see that Terry is tense but doing his best to stay calm and not show it.

The point begins, and the rally is long and ferocious. The girls are hitting the ball unbelievably well. Suddenly Stacey spots an opening on her opponent's court and takes the chance, a very courageous risk. If she makes it, she wins the point; if not, she misses the chance to break. It's a long shot; this opponent serves very well and is seldom broken.

As the ball travels from Stacey's racket, everyone in the stadium gasps and holds their breath. Every eye is focused like a laser on the ball. It clips the net and bounces twice on top of the net; no one knows on which side it will drop. When it spills over onto the opponent's side, Stacey wins the point and the game. The score is 5–4, which means Stacey will be coming out to serve for the match.

The next minute-and-a-half seems like an eternity. No one says much until the girls get up from the chairs to take their respective places on the court. "Come on, Stacey, you can do this," the crowd shouts. Stacey looks at me; with a gentle smile and laser vision, I nod my head in approval showing her I am right there with her.

After three huge serves, Stacey has three match points. She serves again, and the challenger hits a winner. Second match point and our opponent has loosened up and is now just hitting the ball without trying to control it. The pressure is on Stacey. One more match point, and Stacey looks at me. I point to my heart to remind her where she can find the answer. She turns around and walks to the side of the baseline where she will be serving. She tosses the ball in the air and winds up her body, and I know there is a huge serve coming. She strikes the ball in a way that can only be done when a player is flowing in complete harmony, fully there and present in the moment.

"Game set and match," the chair umpire calls as the crowd leaps to its feet and erupts into cheers.

Stacey throws up her arms and turns around to look over at Terry and me. Finally letting out all his nervous energy, Terry shouts so loudly I feel like my ears are going to fall off. This is an amazing moment, leaving me practically speechless.

Stacey runs over to me and Terry and embraces us. "Let's enjoy the moment, hey?" she says with a huge smile before turning around and running back to the place where the awards will be presented.

The triumphant Stacey receives her trophy and check. The match officials hand her the microphone to say a few words. She glances at the ground, briefly gathering her thoughts. Then she looks out at the crowd, thanks them for their support and commends her opponent, as goes the customary speech. Then she speaks of how she and I have been working together, the distance we have come, and the hard work and sacrifice that are now paying off. The crowd claps and cheers.

As we walk out of the stadium, my phone rings. It's my dad. "Pablo! Wow, that was amazing! Congratulations, son," he says.

"Thanks, Dad. I hope you enjoyed it from there," I reply.

"Are you kidding me? I enjoyed every minute of it," he replies.

The two of us recap the highlights for a minute or two as he has watched the match on television. As we talk, I yearn to be with him, something I have not felt since I was a young child living at home.

"You need to go see him, Pablo," I hear God whisper into my heart as I end the call.

Lord, you are so right, I think. *You will have to help me find the time to do it.*

As Terry and I reunite with Stacey, we embrace her and each other. This is a very special moment for all of us.

"Stacey, I am so proud of you," I say. "But more than that, I am thrilled to have heard the words you said out there today."

"Pablo, I could not have done it without you coming in and telling me what you told me at the end of that first set," she replies.

"We told you how very important it is to have the right people around you," I reply smiling broadly.

My mood changes when Terry interrupts. "Pablo, I have to go," he says.

"Oh no, Ter. I thought you were staying another night," I reply.

"There a few things I need to take care of back at home," he says. "Plus, I think my time here has come to an end; I have done what I came to do."

"Terry, if you could stay one more night, I have something on my heart I want to talk to you about. It's been a long time coming," I say.

Noticing the urgency in my voice and perhaps also the pain, he replies, "I'm sorry, Pablo," when he is interrupted by a phone call.

Returning to our conversation after taking the call, Terry says, "I thought you and Stacey would be leaving first thing tomorrow as you normally do. I can take care of the matters back home over the phone. I will stay one more night."

"Thanks, Ter. You don't know what that means to me," I reply. As we walk back to the clubhouse, I search for the words to express what I am feeling inside about my relationship with my dad.

I realize the purpose of this journey was to bring me back to the original transgression, where I could receive the healing which is making me the man I am today. My thoughts turn to God as I say to myself with a smile, *You are not safe, Lord,* remembering C.S. Lewis' *Chronicles of Narnia.*

"No, I am not Pablo." I hear Him whisper in my heart. "But I am good."

Amen. You are very good.

Soon I will find out more than ever before how good He really is.

CHAPTER 11

COMING HOME

... but this is a wonderful time, and we had to celebrate. This brother of yours was dead, and he's alive! He was lost, and he's found!'"

—Luke 15:32

Deep calls to deep at the roar of your waterfalls; all your breakers and your waves have gone over me. By day the LORD commands his steadfast love, and at night his song is with me, a prayer to the God of my life.

—Psalm 42:7–8

"So what's up, Pablo?" Terry asks as we sit down in the clubhouse couches.

"It's my dad, Terry," I reply. "I can see it was no accident
he turned up here unannounced. I know God brought him here
intentionally.

"As I spoke with him last night before he left, I realized how
much I love him as well as how much I hold against him. It's
the first time I've been able to feel both sentiments simultaneously. Previously I either felt affection for him or resentment.
The affection usually came to an end when resentment set in,"
I explained.

"The thing is, Terry, I don't know how to resolve this and
how to tell my dad about it. I don't want to hurt him, but at
the same time I feel it is time I laid down the resentment and
allowed God to heal me and set me free. I expect the healing
will require talking honestly to my dad," I say.

People are slowly clearing the hall where we are sitting,
and volunteers are packing up equipment at the same time
as the TV staff are packing up audio and video gear. One
tournament is over, but I sense another is just starting in my
personal life.

Noticing Stacey heading our way, I try to put the brakes on
our conversation. "Terry, Stacey is coming," I say.

"Pablo, if you are okay with this, I think we should invite
Stacey into our conversation. It will help her to see and hear
what you have to say," Terry advises, looking me in the eye.

"Yeah, I guess that's okay," I reply hesitantly.

Terry and I both stand up to greet Stacey as she arrives with her bags and her trophy. "Well-done, Champ! I'm so proud of you," I tell her.

"Yeah! Well-done, Stacey. You were superb today," Terry adds.

"Guys, I still have to go and meet the press. I already did my cool-down and stretching, so I should be back in about half an hour," she says.

"That's fine, Stacey. Take your time as Terry and I have plenty to talk about," I say with a cheeky smile on my face.

As she walks away, Terry asks, "Pablo, can I share how I dealt with a similar situation with my dad a few years back?"

"Sure, Ter," I reply.

"Like you, I came full circle and realized I had to take care of business with my father. I realized that almost everyone has issues with their parents; they all fall short of expectations, somehow. In reality, they usually try their best, but they still end up treating us the way they were treated by their parents," he says. "No one can give what they don't have, and that holds true for our parents.

"But you and I have an amazing position of privilege," Terry continues. "Because of what God has done in our hearts, we are in a position to do for our dads what they could not do for us.

"Pablo, you give affirmation to those around you every day, but you never got any for yourself, especially from your dad," Terry says, speaking softly. "What you have done with Stacey is incredible."

As he says this, something erupts in me. Tears flood down my cheeks like a waterfall, and my insides moan and groan like a newborn child. Terry's words are like water to an area of my life that is as dry as the Kalahari Desert.

"Thank you for noticing, mate," I reply with a breaking voice as I wipe tears off my face. "Just as you did, I always wanted to please my dad. I guess we all want to see our dads smile and approve of us. But I always felt dad was never happy, like I never quite made it. I believed that if I were simply to be myself he would be disappointed in me. I always tried to be someone I was not in order to impress him, and eventually this spilled over into other relationships.

"I have come to realize that I have been living someone else's life, trying to meet expectations I thought someone else had of me. But now I know that God wants me to be myself and no one else. To be myself and live in relationship with Him and with the people He puts in my life—this is where the true treasures in life are found."

"Pablo, you need to talk with your father," Terry says.

"God has told me to go see him," I reply. "I realize that the relationship with my dad is at the root of my issues. God is leading me back to where the hiding and pretending began; it is from there that I became the driven man I was. The work God has been doing in my life has been preparing me to return to the place of the original pain," I tell Terry, as it is all so clear to me now. *Why didn't I see this before?* I wonder.

"Because you are seeing with the eyes of your heart now, Pablo, whereas you weren't before," God gently reminds me.

Stacey returns, and she and I say good-bye to Terry. I am amazed at how all three of us have been on this journey together in a way I never could have orchestrated. As we embrace, I sense my time with Stacey is coming to an end.

Fans are waiting to have their photo taken with Stacey, so she poses for several pictures before we walk Terry to his car in the parking lot. Stacey and I request a courtesy car to take us back to the hotel.

On the way there, Stacey shares how spectacular she feels inside and how grateful she is for this moment. When we reach the hotel, the two of us talk outside for awhile.

"Stacey, I want you to know I am extremely proud of you and the way you have progressed. Thank you for trusting me. Thank you for believing in my abilities as a coach and entrusting your career to me. It has not always been easy, but I have enjoyed it all nevertheless," I say, as we laugh together.

"I have been thinking about the future, and I would like to take off these next few weeks. Now that it's the end of the year, I would like to take some time to think about what we should do next year."

I can see Stacey is not happy about what I am saying, but at the same time I know she is quite capable of going on without me should that situation arise.

"Okay, Pablo, that's fine. I understand," she replies. "Thank you for everything, and let's stay in touch." We get up from our chairs and embrace.

As we walk away, I am overcome with the thought that this might be the last time we speak as player and coach. I feel a great sadness, but I choose to rest in knowing that God will work out everything in a way that will be the best for both of us.

I turn my thoughts toward going to see my dad and regaining the place in my heart held captive for far too long by the wounds of the past. I am ready to walk into the pain and the storm raging within me for as long as I can remember. That very broken place has been limiting me in my relationships with God and others.

A couple days later, I'm at the airport, and I write an email to my father telling him I would like to come visit him in the next few weeks if possible. I explain that I have much to tell him and would love the opportunity to do it in person.

I spend the next two hours surfing the net, and before I log off I receive a reply from my dad. To my great delight, he says he can't wait to see me. With a huge smile overtaking my face, I reply that I will let him know the exact time and date of my arrival as soon as I make my travel plans.

Before I board the plane heading home, I email my travel agent asking him to book a flight to South America for me—after my scheduled trip to South Africa to visit my children.

On the way to South America, I realize it has been a very long time since I have visited my home country. Naturally, I am filled with feelings of nostalgia.

"Hey, Dad!," I yell, throwing my arms around him upon meeting him in the airport.

"It's good to see you son," he replies. "How was your flight?

"It was great. I slept all the way," I tell him as we head to the car.

On the way to Dad's home, I notice so much that has changed since my last visit. There are so many new buildings that I don't even recognize some places. *Gosh, I have been gone for a long time,* I think as rows of buildings and houses flash by.

During our conversation in the car, I realize this visit is going to be like no other. I have so much I want to say to my dad, but at this point I don't know how, when or where I will say it. Yet slowly I become more relaxed, holding on loosely, and happy to let God show me the right time and place. I have no idea that an incident in store for us will prompt all the details to fall into place.

We arrive at Dad's apartment and greet the woman he is dating, as well as the maid he has had for years.

"Pablo, did you bring the DVDs with the photos I asked for?" Dad inquires.

"Yes, I did, Dad," I reply.

"Do you mind if I go down to the shop with my girlfriend to get them copied while you get a shower?" he asks.

"Dad, would you mind if I go with you guys?" I reply, handing him the DVDs.

"No, not at all."

"Okay, let me shower quickly, and then we can go."

There is no elevator in the building, so we have no choice but taking the stairs. I'm thankful Dad's apartment is on the fourth floor, not higher. On the way down, I notice the stairs are somewhat slippery, so I warn my father, his dating partner and also the maid who is going out to buy some milk.

When we reach the last set of stairs and the lobby is in sight, my dad lets go of the handrail. He suddenly disappears from my view, and the next thing I know he is rolling down the stairs.

I rush down to see if he is okay. He stands up briefly but then passes out, falling to the ground and hitting his head on the way down. The people in the building lobby begin to panic. A woman who saw the whole thing is screaming, and by now Dad's girlfriend is crying and shouting too.

With all that is going on around me, I stand looking at my father who is on the ground and not breathing. He is literally dying in front of my very eyes. People trained to deal with situations like this, and who should be handling this one, are panicking too. Yet I sense a deep stillness within me as I remain in the moment.

I kneel down beside my father and discover that he can't breathe because his tongue is blocking his airway. I gently turn him over and realize the side of his head that hit the floor is very swollen. "Have you called an ambulance?" I ask his girlfriend.

"Yes, they are on the way" she replies, shaken.

"On my gosh, Pablo! Your dad!" the maid says, covering her mouth and visibly in shock.

"It's okay, Ricardina. Calm down. He is going to be fine," I reply.

"Dad, breathe," I say, as my father begins to gasp for air, visibly struggling. The ambulance arrives, and the EMTs take over as I brief them on what has happened. They move my father into the ambulance.

I hear my father calling my name to see if I am there with him, as I climb on board the ambulance and again at the hospital as the EMTs wheel him into the emergency unit.

"Pablo, please stay with me," he says, grabbing my hand.

"I am here, Dad. Don't worry. I am not going anywhere," I reassure him.

After all the necessary tests have been done, the doctor tells us my dad will be okay. "You need to thank this young man for staying calm and helping you start breathing again. If he hadn't, it may have cost you your life, sir," the doctor says.

Smiling at my dad and not knowing what to say, I realize my calm reaction was made possible by the changes which have taken place within me over the past few years, teaching me to stay in the moment.

My father must stay in the hospital for a day or two, mainly as a precaution to be sure that the swelling goes down and there are no blood clots in his head.

"Pablo, I don't want to stay here on my own," he says.

"You won't have to, Dad," I reply. "I will go get some dinner and then come back with your girlfriend."

While a couple of nurses take care of my dad, I go to meet his girlfriend, who has driven to the hospital.

"How is he, Pablo?" she asks.

"He is okay," I reply. "He is going to be fine, he just needs to stay put for a couple of days to make sure there is no swelling or clots in his head."

As we sit down to eat dinner, his girlfriend asks, "Pablo, how could you be so calm seeing your dad lying on the floor dying while everyone else was panicking around you?"

"Oh, I guess it's practice," I reply, smiling. Inside I know this is not the truth, yet I am reluctant to get into a full explanation of staying in the moment—how you are more likely to do the right thing when you focus on what is happening without going anywhere else in your mind.

After dinner, his girlfriend and I return to the hospital. My father is asleep now, so she says good-night and returns home as she has family she needs to care for there.

I say good-bye to her and enter my dad's room. The nurse tells me he is doing well and has been asleep for a bit. She shows me the bed where I will be sleeping, then she leaves the room.

At 6 a.m., my alarm goes off. I wake up to find my dad already sitting up in bed.

"Good morning, Pablo," he says.

"Hey, Dad, how are you feeling?" I ask him, approaching the bed to give him a kiss.

"I am feeling much better," he says, as the doctor enters the room to examine him.

"You start early," I say, greeting the doctor.

"Yes, we are busy, so I need to start the rounds early," he replies.

My dad receives a good report. The swelling has gone down considerably, and he will be able to return home in the afternoon.

As the doctor leaves the room, I turn to my dad and he says, with tears in his eyes, "Pablo, thank you for saving my life yesterday."

"Dad, I love you, and I am glad I had the privilege to be there to help," I reply, embracing him and suspecting that something has happened inside him through all of this. I will find out after we left the hospital that I am right.

While the hospital staff is running the last tests, I begin to think about how and when to have the conversation I came here for. I decide I will take Dad to lunch at a place close to his home, a place where we will be able to spend some private time together.

The time comes for Dad to leave the hospital. As my dad and I get into the car, I think about the lunch I am planning with him tomorrow and wonder how I will do what Terry suggested. *How will I give my dad what he could not give me?*

"I will help you," I hear in my heart. Immediately I feel a surge of confidence. God has a plan for this conversation and He will make sure it accomplishes all that He intends.

Yes, Father, I need to just hold on loosely and let you take care of the outcome, I reply, whispering under my breath.

Arriving back at my Dad's place, I thank our driver, then help my father up the stairs and to his room. As he settles in to rest, I go downstairs to get something to drink.

I spend the next few hours with God. My mind is full of thoughts about all that is happening, and my heart is aching. I feel that a large part of me is exposed and vulnerable, and I realize that it is the wound I have been running away from all these years. God has stripped away the false protection I have built up so He can bring true healing.

God has been working to bring me back to this place, to the root cause of the disease in my life. The symptoms of this disease have shown up as religion, fears, and most of all, a never-ending need to earn the approval of men and God.

I am amazed how every time I see my dad now I feel compassion and love for him. I am no longer held captive by his offenses against me, but I am overcome by this extraordinary love for him. The resentment I have felt in the past is losing its momentum like a car running out of fuel. I am on my way to healing.

Feeling both nervous and excited about tomorrow's lunch, I return to my dad's room.

"Hey, Dad, how are you?" I say, reaching out to hug him and kiss him on the cheek.

"Good, Pablo. I am glad to be home. I thought I might never get out of that hospital," he replies.

My attention shifts to our lunch tomorrow and my concerns about it. "Stay in the moment, Pablo," I hear whispered in my heart.

Yes, you are right, Lord. I need to just enjoy this moment. The result and outcome of tomorrow are not for me to worry about.

"Dad, you keep relaxing here. I am going for a walk on the beach and will be back in a bit," I say.

"Okay, but don't be too long," he replies.

"I won't. Don't worry."

What a beautiful day, I think as I step into the sand and listen to the waves gently breaking on the shore. The sea is a beautiful green, and the sky looks like it has been freshly painted. There is a very gentle breeze around me, and I feel extremely close to God.

Tomorrow is a big day, Lord.

As I continue to walk and look at the ocean and all the beauty surrounding me, I appreciate the wonder of God's creation. I sense God reminding me that He put all this together, so He can easily handle the lunch conversation with my dad tomorrow.

I sit down on the beach facing the ocean, and as far as I can see, I am the only one on the beach. I feel a mysterious Presence within and around me. I know who it is, and I sense He is in a playful mood. The impression is hard to describe, but I think He wants to dance and celebrate with me.

"I have been waiting a long time for this moment, Pablo," God whispers into my heart.

I smile and laugh. *You are like a big kid. Why couldn't I see this in You before?* I ask.

"Because today you are seeing me with your heart," He says. "In the past you saw me with your mind and your own understanding. It is impossible to know me with your intellect. You can only know *about* me in your mind. Your heart is my domain, that's where I live, and that's where you get to know Me, to know who I am and what I am like. It's in your heart that you experience the *real* Me and not the one others talk about," He continues.

"For too long, you have thought that your heart was not good enough. You focused on your behavior, making a huge effort to act the way you thought I expected you to act.

"I will always challenge you to move deeper into your heart. When you reach a place you think is the deepest you can go, I will call to you from a deeper place and invite you to join Me there. I have much to show you. Your heart is a well with deep waters, and it's by understanding who I am and how I love you that you are able to draw the water out," He explains.

"The world is always pushing you to be someone you are not, to stop you from being yourself. All I ever wanted for you is to just be you. To be who I made you to be and no one else. You are everything you need to be to fulfill My calling for you, the reason I made you," He says.

I feel on the verge of exploding with joy and an exhilarating feeling I can't even put into words. It is as if He is inspiring me to dance. So I get up—no, I jump up—and spin around, my arms open and my eyes closed. And suddenly I feel like I am dancing with my Maker. The waves seem to follow us and so does the breeze. The dance is clearly an outward expression of what is going on inside my heart, and I don't want this moment to end.

I slow down and sit back down on the beach. I look at my watch. I have danced and shouted for more than half an hour, and I have been here on the beach for two hours. *Lord, I have to go back. My dad is waiting.*

With every step I take toward my dad's apartment, I have more confidence that everything will work out fine tomorrow. In fact, I am excitedly awaiting it.

My cell phone rings; Terry is calling. Knowing I have come home to talk with my father, he is supporting me by calling me each day. He reminds me that he will be praying for our lunch conversation.

Back at my dad's place, I go to his room and greet him. "Hey, Dad!"

"Hey, Pablo," he replies. "Where have you been for two hours?" he asks as he sits up in his bed.

"Oh, here and there. I have recovered a sense of wonder, which as you know I had lost altogether," I reply.

It's amazing how I delight in wonder today when in the past I saw it as a total waste of time. My mind was so focused on getting things done and achieving that it seemed ridiculous to spend time in wonder. Yet today these are the times when I have the richest encounters with God.

"Did you get mail?" my dad asks, seeing the envelope in my hand which contains the letter I have prepared to give him after lunch tomorrow.

"No, these are notes I made while I spent time on the beach," I reply, hoping he would not inquire any further about the envelope.

At dinner, I tell my father I want to take him to lunch tomorrow at a very nice place by the beach, not far from his building. Thankfully, he agrees to it. We spend the rest of the evening reading papers and relaxing.

The day I have greatly anticipated arrives. After sleeping in, Dad and I have breakfast together, but I can't stop thinking about our lunch. I am so excited. I have booked a private room and ordered a taxi to pick us up so Dad doesn't have to walk.

We take the short drive to the restaurant, and as we arrive I pay the cab. "Dad, wait for me as I want us to go in together," I say as the driver gets my change.

"There you go, sir," he says.

"Thank you very much," I reply.

The short walk from the taxi stop seems longer today than it has ever seemed before.

"Dad, I am so glad you came and that we are going to share this lunch together today," I say, putting my arm around him. He looks at me and smiles.

The excitement inside me grows with each step we take. By the time we finally reach the stairs and the restaurant entrance, my heart is pounding.

The doorman greets us and opens the door.

"Hello, sir, and welcome," the hostess says to both of us. "Do you have a reservation?"

"Yes, we do. It's Mr. Giacopelli," I reply.

"Oh, yes," she says with a great smile. "Please come with me." She turns around and shows us to the room where we will be having lunch.

"Pablo, why don't we sit here by the window?" my dad asks.

I smile and tell him there is a better place. We stop about 10 meters from what looks like a very small conference room. Its double doors are closed.

"You are in there, sir," the hostess says, pointing to the doors.

"Thank you very much," I reply. A picture flashes through my mind, and I realize this small room is a representation of my heart. I am about to enter a place in my heart that has been closed for many years, and I am entering there with the very person responsible for the wound that shut it down.

The restaurant is very busy, and there are people at every table. I look at my father and ask, "Shall we, Dad?"

We walk toward our private room, and as we get near the doors, I reach out and take my father's hand. Healing awaits us inside this room. My heart is pounding from the excitement of the moment. I am about to have the awesome privilege to do for my dad what he couldn't do for me all those years ago.

Opening the doors, we are hit with the simply amazing view. Framed by trees just outside the windows is the oceanscape, running as far as the eye can see. This is truly a magnificent place for an occasion like this.

As we choose our selections from the menu, I am sure to avoid prawns as my father is very allergic to them. The last thing I need right now is another unexpected trip to the hospital.

We enjoy a wonderful meal, talking and laughing together. When the highly anticipated moment arrives, I whisper a prayer to God. *Father, help me,* I say silently, while recognizing this is such an amazing God-moment that nothing can stop me now from hitting the healing home run.

"Dad, thank you for coming today," I begin. "I have a few things I would like to say to you, if that's okay."

"Yes, of course, Pablo. Go ahead," he replies.

"For me this day is about celebrating and honoring you, Dad, for who you are and who you have always tried to be in my life.

"Some time ago on a trip to South Africa to see my kids, we enjoyed a great dinner together the night before I had to leave. I did not allow my mind to wander into the past or the future but fully enjoyed each passing moment. Today, I want to do the same with you as I speak to you.

"Dad, I know you loved me throughout my life as best you could. There were painful moments in our relationship, but these were not your fault, as you gave to me in the same way you had received.

"I remember all those years back when I was a kid and how I wish our time together would have been different, that we would have had more time to spend together. I wish I would have known then what I know now; but because I didn't, I filled all my time trying to earn your love. How I wish I would have known that you loved me for who I was, that your affections didn't depend on my behavior and performance.

"You see, Dad, I realized on the visit with my kids that trying harder was never the answer as I had thought. I learned that the answer lies in surrendering to God and holding on to life loosely."

The room is dead silent, and my gaze is firmly fixed on my dad. He is stone faced, but I can see in his glassy eyes that he is hearing my words with his heart.

"Today our homes are geographically distant, but the physical distance is not the only one separating us. The consequences of our actions all those years back have prevented us from having the relationship I know in my heart that both of us have always wanted. We can't change the past, but we can make a difference in how it affects our future.

"For this reason, I would like for us to be more open with each other going forward. I would like to have deeper conversations around the table. I am interested in getting to know and love your heart, Dad, in the same way God knows us and loves our hearts.

"I want to share with you what I have discovered in the last few years and give you the chance to experience the wonderful life I have found. I want to give you all I have been given by my Father in heaven. It's a simple fact of life that we can only give what we ourselves have received.

"Thank you, Dad, for all you have done for me. I am glad God used me to spare your life a few days ago. I am glad you are here today, and I am glad that, from this day on, we will be changed for the better.

"I have spoken today from my heart, and I have a letter here I have written for you. In it you will read what I have said today. I have written it down so the words will remain with you. Every time you open this letter I want you to be reminded that I love you. You are special to me, and as far as I am concerned you are the best father who has ever lived. I love you, Dad. Thank you!"

At that point, I stand up, step over to my father and wrap my arms around him. With tears flowing, we hold onto one another for a long time. Inside every tear I cry, I sense healing flowing. *Thank You, Lord. You are finally putting me back together in the way You always meant me to be.*

Through the tears, the healing and the joy, I sense a growing bond between me and my dad. Once again I whisper a prayer to heaven. *Thank You, Father.*

This time I hear a response. "Thank *you*, Pablo."

Thank me? *For what?*

"For your willingness to trust Me and follow me in this journey."

Years later, when I think back on this monumental day, the rest of the day will be a blur. But one thing remains with me now, and I am sure it always will: If we ever stand a chance to discover the true God, we must hold on loosely and let Him have His way in our hearts.

EPILOGUE

God created us to live in this place we know as the Zone. We cannot enter this place by our own efforts to control and manipulate; I learned this the hard way. When we are controlling and manipulating, fear is usually the fuel in our lives, and as a result, we hold on tightly, leaving no room in our hands for God's good gifts of Life.

In this place, the Zone where we were created to live, the fuel of our lives is God's love. When we are fueled by God's love, we learn to trust Him and loosen our grip on the reins of our lives. As a result, we have room in our hands to receive all that God has planned for us. As the Bible tells us, perfect love casts out all fear.

God created us to stay present and in connection with Him; therefore we will never truly succeed if we attempt to do anything by our own effort. The best way to reach our goals is to surrender them to God and allow Him to guide and direct us to this wonderful place He makes available to us because of His great love for us. This place is open to everyone, not just a chosen few.

In the book of Ezekiel, we read that the Spirit invites Ezekiel to go to the part of the river where his feet can't touch the bottom. In that part of the river, the current will take him wherever it goes. Ezekiel has a choice: either fight the current or flow with it. Not knowing where he will end up, he can try to control where he goes, which in a river is pretty much futile; he can give up the fight altogether and therefore drown; or he can hold on loosely, allowing the current to take him to the good place God has for him. By choosing to hold on loosely, he will be able to stay present, enjoy the ride and savor the process.

God's invitation to us is clear as to where He would prefer us. We can choose to stay safely on the shore. If this is our choice, then this is where we will remain for the rest of our lives. But, like Ezekiel, we are invited into the river which leads to a place of healing.

I believe this is a picture of the journey God intends for all of us, a journey that leads us back to the person He originally created us to be. This is a journey leading to the place where our hearts will find the healing and deliverance we need and crave.

On this journey, we will be challenged and our faith will be stretched and tested. It will not be easy. It's a journey similar to whitewater rafting in many ways. It will take much longer than it should at times because of our attempts to control situations and circumstances. These vain attempts will slow us down and may even set us back on the shore, where we have the false sense of being in control. These setbacks are only keeping us from what our heart longs for most.

The choice is ours: stay where we feel safe or jump into the current. God is found in the depths. In the midst of the storm described in Mark 6:45–52, Jesus showed up when the boat was in the middle of the lake, not on the shore.

Epilogue

In the Bible, we learn that the human heart is a well of very deep waters. Scriptural truths offer Life to those depths in our hearts.

If you want to find this Life, you know now what you need to do: *Hold on loosely.*

Enjoy the ride!

—Pablo

ACKNOWLEDGEMENTS

... By myself I am not large enough to call the whole man into activity.

—C.S. Lewis

How true these words are.

None of us can ever become all we were meant to be without the help and interaction of others. I have come to learn that the biggest sharpeners of my character and life have not been events but people. Whether they attempted to impact my life positively or negatively, nevertheless they were and will continue to be, I suspect, the instrument of choice.

No man has made, or will ever make it, all the way home without the help of others, and this life of mine is no different from yours or any other. I am someone who writes and lives from the heart, and this part of the book is no different. The names that I will mention in the following paragraphs are the names of people who are responsible for the man I am today. The order in which they are mentioned has no relevance to the impact they have had, and some continue to have, in my life. They have all played their part, and no matter how small it was or is, I would not have been whom I am today if their part had not been played out.

I want to start by thanking Al Osle for stepping out of his comfort zone and sharing with me for the first time who Jesus was. To Pastor John Centofanti and his wife Lisa for all those hours of counseling and listening to me in my younger years as a new believer. During our times together, I believe God sowed through your lives seeds in my heart that are still growing today.

To my wife, Madeleine: Thank you for who you are. Thank you for sharing your life and your gifts with me every day. You have helped me to once again believe in myself. Without you, I would never have been able to write this book and do so many other things. I love you now and always will.

To Vanessa, Jake and Mia: You mean the world to me. I carry you in my heart every day of my life. You are the biggest gift God has given me, and I want you, all three, to know that your Daddi is very proud of you. Thank you for sticking by my side and not turning your backs on me when you had every reason to. I love you three more than words can say.

To Mom and Dad: Thank you because you did your best for me. You loved me, and love me, in the same way others loved you. You gave to me what you had, and I know that you did so from your heart, and for this I am indebted to you both for the rest of my life. I love you.

Acknowledgements

To my sister Alejandra: Though we have not spent much time together, I want you to know that I love you and I am glad you are my sister. Thank you for all your support over the years, even when we were on opposite sides of the world.

To my "nearly best friend" Malcolm Watkin Baxter: God knew all those years ago when he arranged for us to meet in Nottingham that my life would never be the same again. Your dedication and commitment to my journey continue to touch me today. I am proud to be able to call you my friend. Thank you for standing by me when many others turned their backs on me. I know now that you were often the presence of God besides me when I travelled through some of the darkest moments of my life.

To my spiritual parents, Colin and Barbara Smith, and their sons Duncan, Russ and Murray: Thank you for being there when no one else was. Thank you for showing me the hands of God in the way that you selflessly gave to my family and me all those years ago. Your example had a tremendous impact on my spirit and I know that today it is still very much a part of the foundation of my life.

To my life coach, Michael Simpson: Thank you for your belief in me and for doing all that you have done for me selflessly. Your example is a beacon to my path, and I want you to know that the work we have done together continues to help me in my journey of discovering who I am.

Wes Roberts, you are one of those sages God has sent into my life to play a major role in helping me become the man that I am today. Thank you for your priceless time and efforts, and the way in which you continue to contribute to my journey.

Vern Hyndman, you have brought a new aroma into my life. Your creativity and wisdom were a major catalyst in writing this book. Thank you for the endless hours on Skype and your direct and real approach to life.

To all the guys in The Noble Heart cyber-community Base Camp: Gary, Jeff, John, Tom H., Tom C., Jerry, Sam, Randy L., Randy S., Bob and the rest of you. Thank you for sharing this journey of the heart with me. Thank you for helping me put this book together. You are my band of brothers and there are no other people I would rather go into battle with than you guys. I love you all.

To Tomas Ruzicka: Though we don't share the same views on everything in life, I am grateful to you for speaking the hard words you did to me all those years back in the UK in that locker room. Without them I would probably still be the man I was back then.

To John Grimshaw: Thank you for being a friend through thick and thin. Thank you for believing in me when others didn't. Your friendship and commitment to me were crucial at a time when it would have been so easy to throw in the towel instead of carrying on.

Kevin Miles, you have been my ally in this journey. Thank you for your patience and belief in my story and me. Thank you for taking a risk with me. It has been an amazing ride and one that has impacted me for the rest of my days.

To my editor, Dawn Stuart, for the brilliant editing job she did and how she encouraged the whole process and me.

To Nolan Abney: Thank you for your help designing my book cover.

Thank you to Frank Gutbrod for his excellent work with the interior design and typesetting.

To Aaron Kerr: My thanks for your excellent and proficient work on my website.

To Jeff Gifford: Thank you for designing a fun and engaging promotional video.

To those of you who aren't mention, but who were there for me in the bad and the good times: Thank you. You know who you are. You will always be in my heart with me. I could never have done it without you.

To those who sought to hurt me, but God used it for my good: Thank you for playing your part too. You contributed enormously towards making me the man I am today.

Finally, to the One who sent all of these amazing people into my path: Your hands and grace were visible through each one of them. Thank you for not giving up on me. For pursuing me and being there when all others turned away. You are my Father, Architect and the Engineer of my life. All that I am, I owe to you.

—Pablo

ABOUT THE AUTHOR

Pablo Giacopelli is a certified personal and professional performance coach by the Coach U Inc. Institution and a member of the International Coaching Federation. He is also a qualified professional tennis coach and has also been trained in sports psychology. He has also undertaken several courses on physical training and personal nutrition. Pablo has traveled around the world, which has helped him to better understand and relate to people of different backgrounds, beliefs and cultures. He speaks four languages. Due to his successful involvement with athletes of both sexes, he is one of very few coaches who understands and knows how to empower men and women working in high performance environments. He has also been a guest speaker at many conferences around the world. Pablo is married to Madeleine and lives in Tel Aviv, Israel. He is the father of four children Vanessa, Jake, Mia and Gisella.

Visit Pablo's website at www.holdingonloosely.com.

Want more on living the message in *Holding On Loosely*? A free, downloadable PDF of the *Holding On Loosely Study Guide* is available at www.holdingonloosely.com.